STOP PULLING THE SHIP!

GO FROM GETTING THINGS DONE TO MAKING THINGS HAPPEN —TRANSFORM YOURSELF, YOUR TEAM, AND YOUR APPROACH TO LEADERSHIP

MATTHEW A. OVERLUND

Stop Pulling the Ship!

Go from Getting Things Done to Making Things Happen —

Transform Yourself, Your Team, and Your Approach to Leadership

———

———

Paperback ISBN: 978-1-7343413-0-0

Digital ISBN: 978-1-7343413-1-7

PRAISE & REVIEWS

"Matt has aggregated the leadership and management principles and lessons that are the subject of hundreds of various books and personal experience, and distilled them into key components that are specific and applicable to anyone who is transitioning from being the one that gets things done to leading the team that gets things done, and then presented them in a way that is easy-to-read, thought-provoking, and actionable."

- Andrew Rigor, Lieutenant Colonel, U.S. Army

———

"If you are a new, or even relatively new manager striving to do better for your team and ultimately achieve success then this book is for you. It helps lay out the pitfalls for new managers, guides you through ideas, and walks you down the path towards improvement. Matt does a great job of relating the reasons why we struggle so we can see for ourselves what is going on, and does not just blindly give us the instructions.

Truly worth a read — maybe even multiple reads."

- Chris Geier, DevOps Director & Author

———

"Every leader needs a roadmap to help them navigate the intricacies of guiding, managing, and inspiring their team members. What hasn't been easily available until now is access to a roadmap from someone who has been there and done it successfully.

Not only has Mr. Overlund been a tremendous leader to his teams, but he's also now written the go-to guide every leader needs to successfully lead those under their stewardship.

This will quickly become the most recommended book among company leaders, I highly recommend you get yours right away!"

- Honoree Corder, Author & Strategic Book Coach

This book is dedicated to my Grandparents, Chet & Betty Ramsey. They have taught me much about life, both personal and professional, by merely setting an example to which we can all aspire.

SPECIAL INVITATION

I hope you enjoy the book, but even more than that, I look forward to getting to know you as you progress through your leadership journey.

If you want to get early access pricing to my future books, as well as free content specifically targeted to helping you become a more intentional leader, join my reader's list:

https://go.leadwith.vision/readers

———

You can also connect with me on the following social platforms.

LinkedIn

Add a note to the connection request that you read this book, and introduce yourself!

https://linkedin.com/in/matthewoverlund

Facebook

https://fb.me/leadershipandvisioncoaching

PART I

CLEARING THE DECKS

INTRODUCTION

THE UNEXPECTED COST OF SUCCESS

One of the hardest things you will ever learn is the unexpected cost of success.

Yes, you read that right: *the cost of success*.

Of course, failure often has a cost. And, it's a cost we're all too familiar with by the time we reach adulthood. By this point, It's been used to define acceptable actions and help us navigate the perils of merely being alive, by developing well-placed respect for danger or dangerous behavior.

It started as young children, as we learned lessons to keep us safe and free from injury:

Don't climb on that, you might fall.

Don't touch that, you'll burn yourself.

Don't eat that, it's poison — and how did you even get that cupboard open?!

As we get a bit older, we move into activities that are dangerous but generally unavoidable, like driving. Now we're not only responsible for our own actions but those of the people around us. By this time, we've also started to realize that those other people in the world, well, let's just say some of them are just a little bit off. This generally clicks for us when we see someone driving down the wrong side of the road or backing their car out of the building that they just *accidentally* turned into a parking garage by a misplaced confusion of the controls.

Shortly after comes the realization that we are expected to move out of the home of our childhood. That we should not only establish a societally-approved definition of success for our future selves, but then we should already be well on the way to preparing for its eventual achievement.

I'm not a psychologist. Still, it doesn't take a doctorate in human behavior to see a pattern emerging here: we are training ourselves to pursue the things we want, need, or hope to achieve, and we are also training ourselves to avoid failure.

The problem is that you often can't succeed without first failing and learning. You didn't learn to walk without falling down, probably many, many times.

Once you mastered walking, you didn't go back to practicing falling down. You moved on to learning to *run*. You had found something that worked, internalized that, and moved on to the next goal.

That's the contentious relationship: we need the pressure, the motivation, sometimes even the humiliation of failure to learn, but it's ingrained in us from a young age to minimize risky behavior and avoid failure as we pursue success.

How do we achieve this?

We learn what works, and we repeat it. We expand on it, we repurpose it, we teach it to others, and in doing so, learn more about ourselves.

Early in my adult life, I had an experience that taught me something about success that has remained with me to this day, and that has served me well in my professional pursuits and achievements.

This lesson also eventually resulted in a catastrophic failure that forced me to reevaluate who I am both personally and professionally, and ultimately led to the creation of this book.

As I worked through my last year of High School in the mid-1990s, I had a growing feeling that college wasn't for me. Academics had always come relatively easy for me, and I was at the age where I wanted something more challenging than more years spent in school. Ideally, that would be paired with a chance to travel out of my small town and see more of the world.

When I say I come from a small town, I suspect the image this conjures in your mind is probably not accurate. My graduating class had just 24 students, and the combined population of the two neighboring towns that made up the central part of our small community was around 2,000 people.

I knew I needed to figure out at least the near-term direction for my life, and broadening my horizons both literally and figuratively was the most promising opportunity to do just that.

So naturally, this meant I should join the United States Marine Corps. They had the sharpest looking uniforms. While it is a never-ending debate amongst the many former service members across the internet today, they were *clearly just better*.

I say this very tongue-in-cheek, having many friends and family members that have served and continue to serve across all branches. I met my wife when she was serving with the US Navy. Besides the decades of fun we've had teasing each other over our respective service alma maters, you can see that I've now upped the game to a whole new level by liberally borrowing a concept from the Navy to title and structure this book.

I'll try and keep the service-related puns and inside jokes to a minimum!

So this is how I found myself sweating my way through the Third Phase of Marine boot camp in the summer of 1994. For those of you that have never been to beautiful San Diego in the late summer and early fall, it's a gorgeous beach-adjacent destination with excellent weather. If you are lucky enough to be there on vacation, you can spend the days lazing on the beach and sipping cold drinks.

My experience was not that.

Marine Bootcamp involves a lot of Physical Training (PT), which is code for *lots and lots of running*. Then there is Incentive Training (IT). This generally means impromptu sessions of plyometrics done indoors or out, whenever the mood or need strikes your Drill Instructors. If you've ever subjected yourself to high-intensity training programs that rely on lots of exercises that involve core work, getting up and down off the floor for no logical reason, and generally pushing your body to learn new thresholds for pain, you've got the idea.

Just add some sand and make sure it's sweltering. Think 20 to 30 dudes crammed into a 15x15 foot space and sweating profusely kind of hot.

The Recruit Training Depot in San Diego just happens to be positioned ironically close to the San Diego Airport. For most of your three months of training, your Drill Instructors will briefly pause whatever activity they are currently using for training to watch planes fly overhead. They do this to make you question your life choices. At their insistence, you look up and observe the aircraft flying a few hundred people to some far-away destination. Of course, they take this opportunity to ask the group of sweaty, suffering young men how much they wish they were on that plane. I do not think this real estate selection was at all accidental.

As a Marine-in-training, you progress through three phases. If you survive intact through each stage and successfully pass the required areas of testing, you graduate and earn that coveted title: US Marine. 25 years later, I still feel just as proud as I did on graduation day. It doesn't fade with time, which may put into perspective the difficulty involved in earning it.

What happens if you fail some crucial part of the training? The Marine Corps has regulations, policies, and procedures for everything, and this is no exception.

Recruits that fail or are otherwise unable to complete any component of training are dropped. This means you rotate out of your current training platoon and join the next available platoon in a later cycle to repeat the exercises again. This remediation will continue until you pass successfully, or wash out and go home. Preference is given for the former, of course. Don't get the idea that deciding you've made a horrible, horrible error in judgment is an acceptable option.

One facet of the Third Phase is something of a break in the norm for the senior recruits that are so close to graduation: they are assigned to Service Week.

After many weeks of intense training, you spend a full week basically doing various jobs around the base. You might work in the kitchens, you might do maintenance around the base, you'll definitely clean wherever you get assigned. If you enlisted in any service and managed to get through your time without learning your way around a mop, I'd love to hear the story.

Don't get me wrong, it's still a week of highly structured activity. The Drill Instructors always make time to have a bit of fun with you, you continue to train, but you're also recharging for that last critical sprint to the finish line.

Once service week is completed, you have to pass all the final tests on your way to finally earning what you've been working so hard for over the last 3 months: Becoming a US Marine, officially and forever.

Final Drill, Final Physical Fitness Test, Final Inspection in front of the commander for the Recruit Training Regiment.

So Service Week turns down the heat, metaphorically at least. If you were working in the kitchens, as I did, the temperatures typical for San Diego in late fall are still quite warm for a kid from the Oregon high desert.

Two or three days before Service Week ended for my platoon, disaster strikes.

I find myself at medical because I've developed a cough, feel like I probably have a fever and I'm just generally feeling awful. The doc says I have pneumonia, with an accompanying temperature of 102 degrees.

Who knew you could get pneumonia in San Diego in October?

So my week of low-key service activities comes to an early and unplanned screeching halt as I'm restricted to the barracks and instructed to sleep it off and try not to die without permission.

Fast forward to the end of the weekend. It's Sunday night, the day before the platoon recommences training. We're scheduled to run our final Physical Fitness Test the next day. This is a 3-mile run, 2 minutes of sit-ups, and as an untimed set of dead hang pull-ups.

A perfect score for men of my age group at the time: 18:00 minutes or faster on the run, 80 or more sit-ups in the allotted time, and at least 20 pull-ups.

Obviously, there were less demanding requirements for passing scores. Still, if you've ever had a conversation with any Marine since the advent of the Physical Fitness Test, you probably aren't surprised to hear that the only acceptable score is perfect.

I'm sleeping relatively soundly since I'm still on bed rest, which automatically means I'm off the roster for fire watch in the middle of the night. There's at least a somewhat lower chance the Drill Instructor would choose me should they need a participant in any ad-hoc group training amusements.

At 0200, I'm proven wrong as I wake to a voice near my ear saying my name. Of course, as I open my eyes, every recruit's worst nightmare comes to life. I see nothing other than one of the Staff Sergeants squatting down next to my rack, staring intently at the side of my head at a very uncomfortable distance of about 2 inches.

There are generally 3 or 4 Drill Instructors (DIs) that remain with your platoon for the duration of your training. Each of these has a different role to play or persona. There's the Senior, whose tough but fair and often takes a nearly parental role with the recruits. Then there's the "heavy" — an experienced DI that is tasked with being the primary disciplinarian. He is the master of Incentive Training, and quite likely the source of the most significant percentage of training-induced pain you've ever experienced in your life.

And he's staring right at me.

It's like the scene from Back to the Future when Principal Strictland confronts the always tardy Marty McFly in the hallway and berates him for being a slacker, getting closer and closer to his face until their noses nearly touch.

Let me assure you, this experience did not have the decidedly John Hughes 80's coming of age comedy feel to it.

The iconic "Smoky Bear" hat the Marine Drill Instructors wear is unmistakable. By this point in your training, every Marine Recruit is convinced that any DI that is so inclined could quickly end your pathetic existence with its sharp edge.

My immediate reaction is conflicting instructions from my brain to jump out of bed and stand at attention, or lie very still and hope I'm dreaming and he eventually goes away. I went with the latter, but unfortunately, he didn't leave, and I wasn't dreaming. Worse yet, he started to speak.

"Tomorrow is Final PFT. You are still on bed rest, which means you stay here, and at the end of the week, you get dropped to repeat the third phase over again with the next platoon that picks up."

Yep, this is definitely a nightmare.

"Medical says you can't PT, so when we form up tomorrow, you'll stay here. If you fall in for PT tomorrow, Senior will ask you if you are still on light duty. If you confirm that you are, he'll tell you to fall out, and we will drop you."

"We don't have time to check the status of 90 recruits every day. If you fall in for PFT and Senior asks about your light-duty, maybe we've got the dates wrong? It's up to you."

With that, he leaves. The next morning when the platoon falls in to go for final PFT, I fall in with them.

Senior says, "Recruit Overlund, aren't you on bed rest?"

"No, Sir!"

"Very well, carry on."

So I ran 3 miles. I completed 20 pull-ups. I even suffered

through 80 sit-ups. It was a painful and utterly unpleasant experience.

If you have never tried to run 3 miles when you have the energy level of a wrung-out dishrag, you know what I'm talking about, but I did it. I graduated with my platoon on schedule.

This single event has stuck with me for the rest of my life.

I learned something from this that has shaped my behaviors every day since.

If you want to be successful, you have to show up.

It may not be easy. It may not even seem sane, but ask yourself: What do you want, and how much do you want it?

Be honest with the answer.

Then take a step forward, or don't. It's your path, it's your choice — and you own the eventual outcome.

I learned this lesson, and I used it to significant effect in my own career, but it also eventually failed me. Or, perhaps a better perspective is that I failed myself, and use this lesson as the vehicle.

You see, I leveraged this commitment and dedication to hard work to drive me towards the vision of what a successful life looked like for me — and it worked until it didn't.

I excelled in roles where I was an individual contributor and even had some success taking on management and leadership responsibilities.

I could generally leverage my work ethic and commit-ment to doing whatever was necessary to get the job done, and my career progressed upwards as a result — therein lies the problem that ultimately led to failure.

I was continuing to work harder, commit more time to

work, and struggling more every day with balancing the need to both produce and manage my team.

I found I couldn't let go of doing the hands-on work that had gotten me where I was, but I also wasn't realizing the full value of the team around me.

The rub, of course, was that what I was doing was working. Sure, it was painful, and my quality of life was suffering both personally and professionally. However, I was still delivering successful results, so why wouldn't I continue?

Do what we know works, it's less risky, it's less prone to failure.

So that is what I did. I kept doing what was working, the personal, and eventually, the professional costs, be damned.

Over time this led to a severe impact on my level of engagement with my work. I continued to do more to achieve more and maintain the upward path of my career. That effort was often not realized, and I found myself asking why I should continue doing what I was doing.

I was working exceptionally long hours, my personal relationships had suffered, and I couldn't justify the individual cost for the professional return, the expected travel along the path to success simply wasn't materializing.

What had always worked in the past, suddenly reached its limit.

The skills and practices that had brought me that far would take me no further.

I had to change to transform my approach to leadership to understand how to serve my teams, to *show up* for them, and not only for me.

Change is hard, transformational change is incredibly hard, but the result is worth the effort.

Let's get started.

1

WHO ARE YOU?

I have a theory about who you are — and maybe even what prompted you to take a closer look at this book.

I don't have any particular skills that give me this insight.

I'm not omniscient, telepathic, nor affiliated with any secret government agencies that may or may not be monitoring you through your home's smart speaker.

What I do have is a very particular set of skills; skills I have acquired over a very long career. Wait... that isn't right either.

Also, I don't have a cool accent.

I'm merely making an educated guess. And I use the word educated loosely. I'm *assuming* that you are where I once was, and you're looking for a better way to move forward because what you are doing right now just isn't working.

Put simply: you need help, guidance, a bit of direction. I get it, I've been there too. We'll get into the problem in a later chapter. For now, let's just talk about you.

You're in some form of a managerial role, and that means you have a team that reports directly to you, or you manage something specific like a project or product, or possibly a combination of the two.

You probably have an exciting title with very authoritative words in it: Director of Synergy, Vice President of Objectives, Positive Outcomes Manager.

Okay, kidding aside. My point is that you are responsible for something bigger than yourself.

People depend on you. You have an impact on the business, on customers, on employees — on people and their livelihood, their lives.

You may have found this book a bit earlier in your journey. You haven't yet moved into a role with higher responsibility, but you want to. It's in your personal plan for your career, and you're smart enough to know what you don't know. Well done.

How did you get into your current role? You earned it. How do I know that? People that fall into high-responsibility roles seemingly by accident instead of by design and intentional achievement are not likely to pick up a book like this.

So I can hazard a guess that you were a rock-star (or is it super-star?) employee that has put in the time required to master your areas of expertise.

You educated yourself either formally or informally, you spent the necessary time practicing and improving your knowledge and skills, and you started to earn recognition as the go-to person when something just needs to be done, done right, and done on time.

Sometimes this meant putting in long hours, either on the job; or in the constant development of skills to ensure you can do the job well. You did that, consistently and without complaint. Okay, maybe it was only *mostly* without complaint. You'll receive no judgment here.

Eventually, you start to earn some recognition for consistently performing at an exceptional and noteworthy level.

Then something else happened. Besides focusing on being great at your job, you started helping the people around you.

A bit of advice here, some well-placed guidance there and the teams or projects you work with started to show an observable pattern: Higher success rates, more consistent output, happier team members.

At this point, you may have had a conversation with one of your managers or an executive that said jokingly, "If only I could clone you...".

Of course, the more straightforward solution to solve that need is to promote you. After all, you've already shown an aptitude for the work and a commitment to making your teams successful.

What could go wrong?

This, of course, works its way into your own expectations of what it is you should be doing when you accept that management role: find a way to clone your capabilities across your team.

In case you skipped the introduction: you quite possibly just tripped on your exceptional performance and fell face-first into the unexpected cost of success. Your behaviors, your effort, your commitment to excelling at your job, all combined to earn you a promotion out of the role you have mastered, and into a position where those same skills alone won't make you successful.

But you have aspirations that are bigger than what you can achieve as an individual contributor.

Maybe, you may want the increase your ability to impact those around you. You like helping people grow and improve, especially in an area where you have in-depth knowledge, and becoming a manager will provide you a means to do that more effectively.

Maybe, you want the ability to have a more substantial impact on the business itself. You want more responsibility to affect the overall trajectory of the organization positively, so you can connect your efforts more closely to the business objective. You believe in what the company does, and you want to take a more significant role in achieving it.

Maybe, you simply want to earn more money. There's nothing wrong with that.

If you are like me and so many others, the truth is a combination of these reasons.

Earl Nightingale describes it best in his audio program **The Strangest Secret:**

> "Your success will always be measured by the quality and quantity of service you render. Most people will tell you that they want to make money without understanding this law. The only people who **make** money work in a mint. The rest of us must **earn** money. This is what causes those who keep looking for something for nothing, or a free ride, to fail in life. Success is not the result of making money; earning money is the result of success, and success is in direct proportion to our service." [1]

We want our work to be meaningful to us, to give us purpose. We want to feel connected to our teams and our colleagues, we want to earn more for our work, knowing that we achieved it by delivering value both to the people around us and business we are engaged in or employed by.

So, whatever your reasons for doing so: you'd decided to pursue a management role.

You get the promotion, only to quickly make a realization — you don't want to be one of those disconnected, micro-managing, bossy typical managers that half the team hates, the other half tolerates — and no one respects.

You probably know just who I mean. The caricature of a manager, the likes of which can quickly spawn enough comedic content to drive years of office-themed satire on the small screen like Michael from *The Office*[2], or a few hours on the big screen with Bill and the Initech team from the movie *Office Space*[3].

I don't want to be like those managers, and I suspect you don't either.

Faced with new challenges, new responsibilities, a new normalized level of stress-inducing expectations, how do we react?

You probably fall back on what you know works — and what worked for you in your previous role was doing a stellar job, as a one-man band — the corporate rock-star — and assisting those around you when you can, as much as you can.

The problem? There are only so many hours in the day.

2

WHAT'S THE PROBLEM?

On day one, as a new manager, you probably started out feeling great. You are on the path to realizing your career goals. You earned this upward move, and you are justifiably proud of yourself.

Shortly after, maybe even before your new title has had enough time to wear down the sharp edges, reality sets in. We realize: this is hard. And not only hard, but hard and unfamiliar.

You're doing what you've always done, but repeating earlier behaviors just aren't translating into the results you are used to achieving.

You're feeling overwhelmed. Frustrated. Overworked. Under-appreciated. Competitive, against your own team — *does that even make any sense?*

You are afraid to fail but unsure of how to succeed.

You find yourself losing confidence in your own abilities, and questioning whether all of your previous achievements were some kind of cosmic accident.

Then you throw reason right out the window and really dive into the self-doubt.

I'm not cut out to be a manager.

I'm failing as a leader and should go back to my previous role.

My team is smart, they're going to focus and apply themselves and before you know it they'll be better than me and take my job.

My projects are going to fail, and I'm going to be fired.

You know you can't be successful if you don't show up, so you set those thoughts aside and start attacking the problem.

I'm going to guess that you've found yourself in one or more of the following common scenarios.

Scenario 1: In the Trenches

You try to lead from the front. You always set the example. You continue working harder and longer hours in an attempt to leave the team space to observe and follow your example. Still, they don't seem to be able to replicate your effort exactly, and the overall performance of the team as a whole continues to degrade.

In this scenario, you're trying to continue being the rockstar contributor and also fill the role of the team leader, willing to get down in the dirt and do the work.

There are many positives here, not least of which is recognizing that as the leader of the team, you are still a part of the team. But as you've probably learned, it can be challenging to get this right and not end up questioning what happened to your life as your work commitments creep ever upwards until you are working so many hours you lose track of what day it is.

Scenario 2: Ready, Fire, Aim!

As you transition into your role as a manager, you stop doing everything you used to do and start assigning and managing tasks. Still, the team isn't doing the work the way you would. Eventually, you fall into the trap of micromanaging every job to completion per your exact specifications and expectations. Or you start doing more and more of the work yourself, and once again wonder what happened to your life.

Your team's purpose, area of expertise, and level of experience will have some bearing on the level of task management that is appropriate; in general, the problem in this scenario is one of rushing ahead without a plan or vision for the future.

Where exactly are you rushing off to, and how do you plan to get there?

Scenario 3: The Emperor's Uncomfortable New Clothes

You may also find yourself struggling with delegating in general. This may be your first attempt at being more direct with people, or giving prescriptive direction and setting expectations from a position of authority.

The fairy tale by Hans Christian Andersen from which this scenario draws its name tells of an emperor that is vain and obsessed with his appearance. A group of weavers promises to make the emperor the most exquisite set of clothes that has ever been worn, crafted from a material that is so magical and exclusive that anyone unfit for their position, lacking intelligence, or generally incompetent will see nothing at all.

Of course, the vain emperor commissions the new

clothes with the weavers then get to work producing. Upon delivery, the emperor is mortified to realize that he can't see the clothes either.

To protect his dignity, he proceeds to continue wearing his invisible clothing, parading around in front of his subjects as if nothing was amiss, rather than admitting he was duped quite thoroughly by weavers.

Eventually, a child points what all the adults of course realize but don't want to admit knowing — the emperor is, in fact, wearing nothing at all. At that point, the cat is out of the proverbial invisible bag.

Being new to delegation can feel as comfortable as parading around naked while trying to maintain some shred of respect for yourself and from your team.

When those tasks you delegate out to the team are not completed on time, not completed correctly, or not completed at all, your confidence in your ability to delegate effectively continues to decline.

Before long, you're just waiting for the team or even worse your own manager to call you out and point out that you really don't know what you are doing. That you are, in fact, not the best thing to happen to management for all of the time, but just another naked person pretending to be wearing the most elegant invisible clothes.

The Root of the Problem

You have the best intentions of finding a balance between developing your team's capabilities and continuing to successfully deliver on the team's mission — you know, the one that *you* are now responsible for.

Whether you struggle with letting go of work, figuring out team direction, delegating in a way that doesn't leave you feeling naked in front of a crowd, or one of any number of scenarios I haven't covered here — the problem is always the same.

You got where you are because you developed your abilities and an inherent commitment to doing the right thing and doing that thing right. You worked hard for that, and that work paid off, you are by your own measure, successful.

When you take that promotion and step into that role managing a team, you don't leave those abilities and that commitment behind. Yet, the means of your success in getting here isn't solving your current problems — and being who you are, you refuse to accept failure.

So, You take up a task here or there, saying, "This is just going to be easier for me to do myself, it's too hard to explain."

You start to pick up slack on missed deliverables and quietly work on it in the late hours of the night to just get it done.

You spend more and more time *communicating in explicit detail* what the team needs to do and when they need to do it.

Before you know it, you find yourself working double hours, consuming quantities of caffeine that call into question if you will ever sleep again, and generally questioning your life choices as your whole world becomes about work.

It's overwhelming. What you may be surprised to learn is that it's not that uncommon.

The Pareto Principle & Pulling the Ship

The Pareto Principle is commonly referred to as the 80/20 rule. This principle proposes that, generally, 80% of our results are produced by 20% of our efforts. [1]

An article by Trent Hamm, on the Human Resources blog at American Express, took this concept even further. Proposing that 20% of your employees require 80% of your time, that 20% of your employees cause 80% of your problems, and that 20% of your employees require 80% of your personnel management time. [2]

Consider the opening scene of the 2012 film adaptation of the play **Les Miserables**, based on Victor Hugo's book of the same name. Jean Valjean is a prisoner in a chain gang tasked with literally pulling a ship into dry dock, step by agonizing step.

That 20% group within many teams within many businesses is pulling the ship. It's a pattern of behavior any organization can easily fall into without intentional leadership and careful management.

Can you see this same pattern in the work your team does?

What about the work you used to do, or may still be doing during your late-night efforts to stay afloat? What about the rock-star members of your own team? Does anyone stand out as pulling the ship?

How did we fall into this trap?

So, Who's Actually Pulling the Ship

I suspect by now, you have realized this already: it used to be me, right now it's you, and it's probably some of the other high-performing individuals that you nod and wave to on the way to and from the coffee machine.

Jim Rohn said, "If you want to be more, you have to become more."[3]

This is sound advice, but the problem I faced, and I suspect you have as well, is that we tend to repeat what works — and what has always worked for you is relying on you.

What you are struggling with now is the realization of your own limitations. There are only so many hours in the day, there is only so much more you can do — and you are suffering from the law of diminishing returns. The cost of adding another hour of effort into your day is many times higher than the value that effort delivers, and your engagement and enjoyment of the work is falling, and falling fast.

We need to break away from the Pareto Principle.

We need to prove the 80/20 rule wrong.

We need a way to change how our team works, how that work is distributed, and how we understand our role as a leader.

You've probably heard the saying: "Many hands make light work." It's been present in the English language from the 1300s, and it provides a simple yet profound point of guidance as we struggle to become effective leaders that head successful teams.

We need to remember that our goal as leaders is not just the successful production of results — our goal is to form and lead a team that produces results.

We need to stop pulling the ship.

3

HOW CAN THIS BOOK HELP?

While effective leadership is a skill you will spend a lifetime mastering, there are critical teachable skills that can position you to be a more effective and successful leader, and pave the way for future growth and improvement.

And make no mistake, while much of what we've explored to this point has focused on management and the move into a managerial role, it is leadership paired with management that provides the path forward.

Our focus in the rest of the book will be to explore that forward path and build the foundational mindset and skills that will serve you well in your current role and into the future.

We Lack Perspective

The problem that most often holds us back is that when we need to change our behavior, usually what stops us is a lack of perspective.

We simply don't know what we don't know.

We can't always see past our own experiences. We need a guide, a coach, or a mentor. My intention is for this book to be that guide for you, a guide-*book* that helps you establish both a workable action plan to effectively lead your teams and a strategy for ongoing growth and improvement into the future.

This book represents the collected guidance that I've been given by my own coaches and mentors, the things I've learned independently through trial and error, and wisdom you only gain from falling down and having to pick yourself back up.

It is the summary of knowledge I wish someone could have handed me when I was in the position you are right now. I hope that you not only find the content useful, action-able, and motivating but that you will, in turn, share it with someone else that can benefit it.

Many hands make light work, and as we all become more, collectively, we cannot help but achieve more together.

A Vision For Your Future

One key area we will explore is the value of identifying, understanding, and communicating our purpose or vision, both for ourselves and for our teams.

Let's skip ahead just a bit and practice that now. I mean honestly, who really likes to wait for anything? Not me.

I'm going to share my vision for you — the future version of you that has read this book, reflected on the content, and asked difficult questions of yourself and tried to give honest answers.

Maybe the future you had some spirited one-sided debates with the page as you reflexively struggle against change — but then pressed on, considered the benefits and possibilities and ventured out of your comfort zone of familiar behavior to try something new.

Let's get acquainted with future you — I'm excited for you to meet them! I'm going to have a little fun here and conduct a quick interview with future you.

My Vision for You

How would you summarize your approach to management?

I recognize that as a manager, and more importantly, as a leader, I have a responsibility to establish a purpose for myself and my team.

This requires that I change how I spend my time and ensuring that I invest in continuous professional development. My team and I will always be asked to address new challenges, and the most effective way to prepare for those challenges is to ensure that I am a valuable resource ready to guide and enable my team's success, both as individuals and as a unit.

I have learned to manage my time by saying no to things that don't align with my values or the current strategic initiatives that support my team's or the organization's long term vision.

I have established a positive culture of success on my team and throughout the organization that recognizes failure as a near term opportunity for learning, and values continuous improvement and successful outcomes over all else. This required a change in thinking to realize that building and maintaining a high-performing successful team is a long game that requires vision, strategy, and a commitment to execution.

How has your approach to management changed or evolved?

I am now confident in my abilities as a leader. This was not always the case, as when I first found myself in a management role, nothing had prepared me for the new types of challenges I would face. I had to step back, gain some perspective on how my role and associated responsibilities had changed. And, to formulate an approach to adapt to those changes.

Concurrent to becoming more confident in my ability to lead, I've had to learn to trust my team and their capabilities. To recognize that I can step back from direct involvement in tasks, and still deliver successful results that align to a well-understood, longer-term purpose and near term goals.

These changes have let me regain control of my day to day, reduce stress levels for myself and my team, and put each of us back in a position where we can control our future by being in control of our present.

I'm proud of my team and their growth, both as individuals and as a unit. I feel like I've made the right decision moving out of an individual contributor role and into management. My day to day now is quite different as I have figured out how to take everything that I excelled at in my previous positions and leverage my team to scale that beyond anything I could have ever achieved alone.

How would you describe the contribution you provide to your team in your role as its leader?

I strive to be a valuable leader for my team every day, helping them achieve their personal, professional and shared team goals.

I do this by staying focused on driving success for the entire team as a unit — we succeed or fail together.

I manage my time effectively to ensure that I'm not sacrificing the potential value I could be bringing to my team by focusing on the wrong things.

An important realization for me was that I am not in competition with my team, but working with them to enable their success. Enabling success for my team will open new opportunities for me, even if I can't envision those opportunities from where I am today. That change in mindset was vital. It helped me remove my own self-imposed limitations and serve my team at an entirely different level.

We all struggle with different things as we strive to improve ourselves, to become something more than we were before. You may already be a natural talent when it comes to delegating work to your team and managing it through to completion. Still, I'm willing to bet at some point in your future you'll have an opportunity to offer advice to someone that finds it difficult or impossible to get right.

You see, my goals for you in this book are first to help you transform from that rock-star individual contributor into a rock-star manager and leader, but we aren't going to stop there.

I want you to become an agent of transformational change within your organization. I want your team to set the bar higher for everyone else, to raise expectations not only of what is possible but is achievable.

And I know you can do it.

The Problem of Employee Engagement

Our focus thus far has been primarily on the results you can realize with a focused and intentional approach to becoming the best manager and leader you can be. Then recognizing that managing a team is a very different skillset from being the star performer on a team.

This alone is a worthwhile and valuable goal for us to undertake. Still, we're nothing if not over-achievers, so let's push it a step further.

Employee engagement is a critical measure for any business, and from your own experience as a manager, and formerly as a team member, you can probably see how your own engagement levels and those of the people on a team affect the outputs of that team.

Consider when you have felt unmotivated, disconnected from work, or dissatisfied with your job. What happens to the quality of your output?

It suffers.

And if that lack of motivation, a feeling of disconnect, or dissatisfaction continues, what happens then?

More suffering. And, we're not talking about a localized effect either. After all, we tend to connect with people more the more time we spend around them. Some people are better than others at compartmentalizing. Still, in general, we humans all tend to carry some level of empathy for those around us — and so when someone on our team is not connected, not happy, that feeling tends to spread.

First, their work suffers, then the output from the team as a whole starts to drop off.

On a broader scale, this leads to retention problems with-in the business or organization. What is an organization, if not a more extensive team structure?

If we manage engagement well, both our own and that of our team as a whole, we can help to solve this problem at an organizational level.

People who understand the purpose in their work will

connect with it in a stronger way than those that do not — and the more connected we are, the more effective we are.

My *purpose* (pun intended) is not to overwhelm you, but to excite you about the possibility.

What if in helping you solve the challenges you face in your journey to becoming a better leader, we could also solve the problem of employee engagement and retention across your whole organization?

We can, and we will. We will do it without any additional effort — because teams that are well led and managed, groups that give meaningful attention to creating an environment that promotes success for everyone make for enjoyable work.

When we are engaged, we naturally do our best work. The same is true of the people around us. People do leave teams and jobs, but it occurs less often than those that depart because they were unhappy.

The goal of this book is not just to help you settle into your role as a new manager by becoming a better leader, but to also solve the problem of employee engagement, one team at a time.

We will do that together by helping you become a better leader and in turn, a more effective manager. First, by changing how you view leadership, then changing how you manage yourself and your team by evaluating and adjusting key behaviors in ways that are simple but highly impactful.

In the final section of the book, armed with your newfound confidence and approach to lead, we'll explore how you can adopt a system for improvement that will ensure you are always prepared to meet new challenges as you evolve and grow as a leader.

4

LEADERSHIP VS. MANAGEMENT

"You manage things, you lead people. We went overboard
on management and forgot about leadership."[1]

— GRACE HOPPER

W e've been exploring the effects of transitioning
from being a team member to being its leader.

In doing that, we've looked at the stresses and struggles
that accompanied that transition. We've established that we
need to find a reasoned and practical approach to meeting
these new challenges, preferably one that has a fair chance
of success.

To bring us to this point, I've been using two concepts
more or less interchangeably: Leadership and Management.
I've purposely left the definition of those terms unspecified.
I want to leave you free to read and interpret them based on
your understanding of the meaning of each, and the context
in which it was used.

We need to establish a common understanding of these
two concepts, the relationship between them, and ulti-

mately why we must embrace both if we want to be successful.

Let's start with the dictionary definitions.

The Oxford English dictionary defines **leadership** as follows:

lead·er·ship (noun)
    the action of leading a group of people or an organization.

And, from the same source, **management** is defined as:

man·age·ment (noun)
    the process of dealing with or controlling things or people.

Something I find interesting in comparing the two definitions is the tone of the language used for each. Reread each explanation, focusing on how each description affects you as consider the concepts against your own role and your position and relationship with your team.

We each interpret things based on our own experiences and opinions. Notice that management by definition and, unfortunately, too often in practice, can be applied equally to things or people.

I don't point this out to imply that management as a set of skills is inherently bad or wrong.

What I would like you to think about is the potential outcome if you were to prioritize developing and practicing a management skillset, to the exclusion of any application of leadership.

Let us expand on the definitions of management and leadership independently. As we consider the capabilities of each, we'll discuss how we can combine them to leverage the best aspects of each.

Management

Management as a skill set provides many tangible and desirable benefits to a team or a business. The output of a well-executed application of management are objective, measurable results that are repeatable, and can be relied on for forecasting and planning.

The successful application of management requires a balance of authority, organization, and decision-making skills necessary to direct the actions of a team toward the accomplishment of well-understood goals and objectives.

Risk is managed and reduced by the tight control and execution of well-defined processes that produce proven results. This can refer to a reduction of risk of failure, or reduction of risk of injuries or accidents, or any other incident with a negative outcome. We limit risk by repeating what works.

Scheduling of work and estimates for completion are established based on past team performance, coupled with close planning of the tasks required to achieve a given output. The more well-managed a team is, the more accurate their ability to forecast performance will be, which results in a more reliable ability to plan effectively.

Management excels at these things, controlling and mitigating risks, understanding throughput, and the ability to schedule. However, the more closely managed a team is, the higher the likelihood that they suffer from a loss of autonomy. With that comes a decrease in the level of engagement.

Management focuses on processes and metrics first and results from those skills second. It is understood that by following defined and tested methods, results can be achieved consistently and reliably.

Leadership

Leadership is generally less objectively measurable as it often related to soft skills and subjective evaluations of behaviors more than tangible and quantifiable outcomes.

The first principal component of leadership is an ability to identify and understand the vision and define goals in alignment with that vision. The definition may be somewhat abstract in nature. The things we seek to achieve that are big enough to qualify as a vision for the future are often big, ambitious, and far from where we are currently.

The best we can do to describe what success looks like is to assume that we'll know it when we get there.

Leadership requires an ability to build and leverage influence and inspiration to guide a group of people to achieve the desired result that is aligned to a well-understood vision.

It requires both a recognition of risk and a willingness to assume that risk. An effective leader must be able to relinquish control in pursuit of larger goals, recognizing that what is achieved is often more important than how something is accomplished.

To be effective, leadership requires relationships to function, and those relationships — like most relationships — are built on trust.

This exchange of trust and relaxing of control allows for the acceptance of risk that is inherently present in the unknown. This is how leadership can achieve goals that are not entirely understood at the outset.

The desired outcome of applied leadership is to change

the behavior of a group of people by encouraging autonomy in pursuit of a prevailing direction that is guided by shared intent.

To do this, leadership focuses on achieving results first, and the process by which those results are achieved second.

The Best of Both Worlds

These are my own interpretations of leadership and management. While I'm making an effort to avoid bias, I'm sure I have not been 100% successful.

I'm confident there are competent, capable managers who can demonstrate how to be an effective manager by mastering and employing management skills alone.

My question to them would be, "Why would you want to?"

Like I said above, I'm admittedly biased, and unashamedly I hope to bring you over to my way of thinking.

Different teams will require a different balance in approach between management and leadership practices depending on their mission or the nature of work they are responsible for. The risk profile, deliverable requirements, and team composition will weigh heavily on this.

Consider a team responsible for delivering life-impacting services like hospital staff in an emergency room, versus the staff providing your lunch at a fast-food restaurant.

The scope, scale, and impact of the work are vastly different, and the tolerance for risk is so dissimilar that it defies comparison.

You may or may not have direct experience working on a team with a life-impacting mission. Either way, it's not much of a stretch to imagine that the focus on risk mitigation is higher. The undeniable need for reliability and consistency in the execution of the team's mission are critically important.

On the surface, this would seem to argue for an approach that favors management practices over leadership. When the cost of failure is so high, shouldn't we mitigate that risk as effectively and successfully as we can?

Of course, we must. But to do so to the exclusion of any focus on leadership, or conversely to move to the other extreme where we fail to give any attention to management, will set us up for failure.

If we err towards an approach that employs management without sufficient leadership, we run the risk of losing engagement on our team.

Engagement is driven by passion, a very people-centric concept. I've yet to observe a passionate process. We must aspire to be professional, but we cannot separate ourselves from our emotional responses. We are human after all — and ultimately, we shouldn't try, as the results would be counterproductive.

Consider the iconic science officer Mr. Spock from the long-running TV and film series Star Trek. Spock was a half-human, half-Vulcan whose character often struggled with the dual nature of his heritage.

The alien Vulcan culture valued logic above all else. Humans are a bit more unpredictable in our behaviors and beliefs. These conflicting elements of Spock's personality often drove the plot via his interactions with Captain Kirk.

As a half-Vulcan, Spock's cultural dedication to embracing logic above all else was always at war with his half-Human emotional nature. Usually, the logic-loving

Vulcan side seemed to win over emotional responses, but what result did this have?

Spock often seemed overly disconnected and dispassionate, especially when compared to his human counterparts.

As managers, I see us making the same mistake when we focus on a management-centric approach to achieving results, ignoring leadership. Whether due to the necessity of risk mitigation or simply because our comfort level with management-oriented skills is higher — the end result will always be the same.

We appear dispassionate, like Spock.

We are disregarding a fundamental fact about our teams: they are comprised of passionate, at times illogical, humans.

When we are connected to the work we are doing, the people we are serving, and the team around us, we remain more engaged. We show up because we care.

It's a mistake to manage this connection out of the equation.

We can, however, err in the other direction. In our desire to lead, to promote autonomy and passion within our team, if we neglect process, neglect measurement, neglect accountability, we run the risk of not just failing, but failing spectacularly.

Leadership or management can drive behavior and deliver results. How you leverage each skill set to achieve that will be very different depending on where your strengths and weaknesses lie.

The key is to find an appropriate balance, lying somewhere between the two extremes.

Management can drive measurable results, but it is leadership that forms organizational culture. A balance is necessary, as neglecting either can be detrimental to the long term effectiveness of the business.

Balancing the two is a unique and rare skill.

A survey conducted by the Harvard Business Review in 2017 confirmed that it is possible to both drive results and build an engaged people-centric team. Interestingly, the people who ranked highly in both leadership and management skills were among the highest-ranked leaders overall. [2]

It is not easy, as evidenced by the relatively small percentage of the surveyed group that exhibited a mastery of each skill set, but it is achievable.

As managers, if we focus exclusively on *getting things done*, we lose our ability to *make things happen*, and we limit ourselves and our team in the process.

Describing yourself as a manager is about what you do: it communicates that you are accountable for the delivery of some objective.

Describing yourself as a leader is about who you are: it says that you focus on enabling and guiding people towards the achievement of an objective.

Conversely, if we don't focus on management enough, we're unlikely to reach the strategic, objective goals by which our team and ourselves are measured.

We have to stop believing that leadership and management are mutually exclusive or that one can or should exist without the other.

We must learn to lead and manage effectively to elevate our team's capabilities beyond their current limitations. This will enable us to leverage the appropriate skills of each discipline to make our teams successful and promote growth over time.

The ultimate result: goals that were previously impossible become clearly achievable.

Leaders Take Action

Let's inventory your impressions of leadership and management:

- Grab a notepad or sheet of paper.
- Create two columns labeled: Leadership and Management.
- In each column, list the descriptive words or activities you associate with the topic.

Set the result aside until you finish the book. After completing the book, review your answers again. How has your view of leadership or management changed?

5

ORGANIZATIONAL CULTURE

WHAT DOES IT MEAN, AND WHY DOES IT MATTER?

As a manager who is trying to find their feet, you may be asking yourself why I've included a complete section on the culture within the organization.

Isn't culture something the executive team, the founder, the president, the CEO, or basically anyone with more authority than me supposed to look after?

Wait a minute — maybe it's in the employee handbook that I *definitely*, *absolutely* read cover to cover.

I hate to be the bearer of bad news, but as a manager — and even as a rank and file employee — you are responsible for organizational culture.

While this is a topic that warrants a complete book of its own, you must recognize the role culture plays in any organization. You must understand how that will influence your own actions as you manage your team.

The common misconception is that we think culture is simply a set of values or rules. Commandments set in stone, chiseled into a giant block of granite and often adorning a prominent wall in the office for all to see.

Behold, our values! (Queue the trumpet fanfare)

There is nothing wrong with this, of course, it's often a beautiful, impressive display.

The problem is that a display alone does not create a working culture.

So, if culture isn't an agreed set of rules of behavior or values, what is it?

Free coffee, soda, and snacks? Providing daily catered meals? On-site laundry services? Sorry, no, that isn't culture, those are just perks. They may be an expression of the company culture, but they don't define it.

Nap pods? Guided meditation sessions? Bring your dog to work day? Again, more perks.

Don't get me wrong I enjoy a lot of these things myself when they are provided. I think that they make great *perks*. What they don't do effectively is help us, as managers, to understand or embody the organizational culture.

My point here is that culture is not what you see represented on TV sitcoms like **Silicon Valley** on HBO[1], or satirical fiction such as **The Big Disruption** that you can read on Medium[2].

The things we talk about most often, even the things we personally identify when asked what we like about our jobs or offices — these things are perks, not culture.

What is culture then?

Culture is the organic, changing environment that occurs when an organization agrees to and adopts a set of shared values in every action they take and every goal they pursue.

Culture will initially be defined as an expression of ideal expectations and values, typically established by the founder. This definition is not always an intentional or formal event.

Culture established by accident is all too common.

This formation of culture will be influenced by beliefs about how business should be conducted. It will often encompass how employees should behave and be treated both in interactions with each other and with customers.

As an organization matures and grows, and mainly as staff changes are made, the culture itself will evolve and manifest itself within the business in different ways. It will adapt to be an outward reflection of the current employee population, and how they interpret the culture as they understand it when they are introduced to it.

Am I trying to imply that the culture is defined by the people, instead of something everyone must accept and abide by?

Absolutely.

Culture is more comparable to a body of water than a block of stone. What happens when you drop a rock into a still pond? It makes a splash, and the result of that action ripples out from the point of impact, reshaping the surface of the water.

Culture behaves similarly, and this is why it can be so difficult to define. It is affected by every change in the organization, large or small.

I can set a cultural ideal. I can enshrine it for all time in the employee handbook, or carve it into the wall of the reception area. It is still only guidance for expected behavior.

Without acceptance and commitment from the people in the organization that they will embody those behaviors or beliefs that describe the culture in their day to day actions, they are just words. A nice thought, at best.

Left unchecked, unmanaged, or in a vacuum of leadership, we can find ourselves with the opposite of accidental culture: an intentional culture that is not recognizable when measured against the original intent.

How do we solve this? Can we work to make an idea become a reality? How do we ensure the culture is not an accident or an intentional deviation?

We lead and encourage our teams to embody the cultural ideal, regardless of how large or small our team may be.

We do this by first recognizing that every person on our team affects the cultural reality around them with every action they take, intentional or not.

This is the additional, sometimes overlooked responsibility you must assume as a manager. More so, as a manager that wants to be successful.

As a manager, you play a pivotal role in the evolution of organizational culture. It cannot be defined and expected to grow without attention.

I'm no gardener, but if I plant seeds in an indoor planter and I never tend them, nothing good will come of it.

You might be saying, "Isn't this something Human Resources should take care of?"

Sure, Human Resources certainly has a role to play. In fact, they probably authored the employee handbook. In a small company, it may even be feasible for the person responsible for the HR function to maintain enough direct interaction with everyone in the business to provide leadership on culture.

This is ideal where it is possible but think back to the founder trying to set the culture and drive its realization alone. It's a job that is too big for any one person or group. The larger the business becomes, the less this approach will work.

Does the HR department attend many of your team

meetings? Do they sit in on your day to day work sessions, or observe your interactions with the customer? What about the CEO or founder?

If your company is small enough, you might be able to answer yes to these questions. What about in the future? How will this scale?

Not well.

I don't say this to imply that executive leadership or Human Resources can have no role in the development of culture, quite the opposite. Their purpose must be to provide guidance on culture. To embody the cultural ideal, they want the company to realize, and act as role models for other leaders within the organization, who then carry that cultural ideal to their teams.

Culture requires regular attention. It needs to be managed, guided toward a desirable outcome, and this guidance comes from leadership throughout the business, and on every team.

As a manager, new or not so new, this falls on you.

You must lead the realization of a sub-culture within your team, and you must align that evolving team culture to the culture of the organization.

Sub-culture? Is that where the team all buys matching shirts at Hot Topic to wear on casual Friday?

Not exactly.

We've discussed how culture is affected by every change in the environment. But, what is our team, if not a micro-environment within the larger organization?

We must realize that our teams will naturally evolve a culture of their own. What is our team, after all, if not a smaller organization, with goals, values, and an inherent personality?

As we work to realize the organizational culture by guiding our

team toward the ideal, we must do so without removing the team's unique perspective and personality. Just as each personnel change will impact the team culture, this interpretation of the cultural ideal will also have an effect on the organizational culture itself.

The relationship is symbiotic.

Culture really does resemble a complex organism with a life of its own.

It also seems like a lot of work to manage effectively.

So, what's the upside?

As we will explore in the rest of this book, as managers that strive not just to manage but lead, one key indicator we need to pay attention to is engagement.

How engaged are we personally in our day to day role as our team's leader? How involved is each member of our team?

Are we excited about the work we are doing?

Do we understand how our work fits into the broader organizational goals or mission?

These are not always easy questions to answer. The answers are sometimes surprising and not always easy to accept.

Engagement is a direct measure of how connected we feel to our jobs, our team, the organization, and the mission. We are all seeking connection and meaning in our work. We want to know that the work we do has value and impact on a larger purpose. When we achieve that, our level of engagement rises, and when we don't, it falls.

Your success as a manager will be directly tied to the success of your team.

If you want an engaged team that consistently produces

exceptional results, you must find a way to energize them. You must find a way to connect them with something bigger than themselves.

They need a purpose.

That purpose doesn't have to be solving world peace. Your challenge will be to connect your team to a goal that is well-aligned to the needs and ideals of the organization.

As a leader, you must understand and embrace the culture of the organization. You must guide your team to align with it while recognizing the importance of your team's sub-culture. This requires an understanding of the discrete differences in how the team will realize the cultural ideals of the organization as their unique team personality develops.

Establishing a thorough understanding of culture and the role it plays within the organization is the first step towards becoming a leader among managers.

———

Leaders Take Action

Free sodas and donuts are an example of organizational culture.

- [ ] TRUE
- [ ] FALSE
- [ ] What? I had to run out for donuts!

PART II

GETTING UNDERWAY

INTRODUCTION

TRANSFORMING YOURSELF

For the first section of this book, you and I needed to get acquainted.

Why?

Well, I'd like you to know a bit about me, at the very least enough that when I throw a completely new idea your way, you're willing to turn it over a few times in your mind and give it some consideration.

That requires a bit of trust.

More importantly, though, I've been writing to you and exploring my understanding of what you're going through. This serves an essential purpose. I want you to understand that I've been right where you are now.

Our situations are sure to be different in their detail, but also quite similar in our shared experiences. This is the book that would have most helped me when I was struggling through the same challenges you are now facing as you find your feet as a leader.

I won't make the claim that everything you will ever need to be the best leader you can be is waiting for you on the next few pages. I will, however, give you everything I can that will set you on that exact path.

I'm going to assume if you're still with me at this point, we're sufficiently acquainted, and you're ready to get to work. So here we go.

In this section, you are the star of the show.

Don't get a big head now — we've got some hard work ahead, and we need to establish a solid foundation of behaviors in our new role as leaders. To do that, I *may* need to throw some proverbial tomatoes in the direction of the stage.

If they happen to hit you, I promise they won't hurt much; my intent is entirely helpful, and I am actually aiming at your limiting beliefs and behaviors.

We're going to dive deep into six critical areas as groundwork for all that lies ahead once we move into Part III: where we shift the focus over to your team.

- **Focus:** We'll explore why you need 100% commitment and attention to every task that is worth your valuable time.
- **Communication:** your career as a manager will be short-lived if you aren't able to effectively make yourself understood.
- **Time management:** Our most precious resource is often the one we squander too much of without really realizing we are doing so.
- **Influence:** The currency of modern leaders has shifted. It is no longer authority alone.
- **Systems:** Documenting and creating systems out of all the things you've mastered so thoroughly that you've forgotten them completely.
- **Failure and Success:** Our relationship with each

is about to change. This is a topic area that we'll cover both here in Part II and again in Part III.

When you finish this section, you'll have everything you need to overcome the feeling that you need to do everything yourself.

You'll recognize the path and growth necessary for you to become an effective leader that can inspire and direct their team such that it becomes greater than the sum of its parts.

6

LEADERS VALUE FOCUS

Multitasking is killing your productivity and performance and may even be damaging to your professional relationships with other people.

I can hear you now:

"Here we go again, someone else telling me to I shouldn't be answering emails during meetings."

Yes, that's what I'm going to tell you. I'm also going to give you some new perspective as to why you should listen and consider a change in behavior.

You might have a problem with multitasking if:

- You started to answer an email while talking on a call and promptly lost your train of thought on both tasks. (I've done this.)
- You began to read and respond to a notification in the middle of a presentation because your phone or smartwatch alerted you to its arrival — the problem is you were the speaker. (I've done this one too.)
- You type, text, and talk at the same time all day,

every day. Clearly, you are a multitasking savant and exempt from all rules, studies, or opinions about how multitasking isn't productive. (Not me! Okay, this used to be me, but I've come around, and I hope you will too).

You may or may not agree with this, as some of the studies can actually be justified towards some specific instances where multitasking can be productive. Tasks that don't require a high degree of focus can be handed off for us to execute almost without thought. This leaves us free to give the majority of our attention to something more deserving of it.

This is how we talk and prepare dinner, listen to a meeting and type out notes at the same time, eat and read, listen to music and write, or some other creative output.

In her 2010 article for Science Magazine, Gisela Telis explained:

"When the brain tries to do two things at once, it divides and conquers, dedicating one-half of our gray matter to each task, new research shows. But forget about adding another mentally taxing task: The work also reveals that the brain can't effectively handle more than two complex, related activities at once."[1]

In every case where we can pull this off successfully, there is a primary task and a secondary task. If you look closer, you'll probably notice that all the secondary functions require less attention.

They are generally things you have entirely mastered both mentally and physically. They aren't mentally taxing.

You are literally on auto-pilot as you execute those tasks, while your primary focus is on other things.

So, how is this a problem?

We've internalized the execution of those secondary tasks by repetition and improvement over time. If we do think about them at all, we are likely to dismiss them as something simple, not worth our attention.

From there, we start thinking about other things of similar complexity. But we also begin to blur the definitions between easy and small, quick, or repetitive tasks.

You know, things like notifications.

How did we fall into this notification driven trap in the first place?

We are inundated by psychological engineering that is explicitly trying to build habitual behaviors and relationships between us and our phones. There's an app for *everything*, and they all send notifications.

While this can be abused by unethical developers, it's not inherently wrong — the intention is to be helpful. Notifications, when used well, are about providing us vital information at the time we are most likely to need it.

Our problem is that we don't tend to regulate ourselves well enough to ensure these notifications are serving their purpose. We let them run rampant and start running our lives. We may even think we have a good reason for that.

In his book **Hooked: How to Build Habit-Forming Products**, Nir Eyal applies the "5 Whys" concept to understand one possible need for real-time notifications:

"WHY #1: WHY WOULD JULIE WANT TO USE EMAIL? ANSWER: So she can send and receive messages.

Why #2: Why would she want to do that? Answer: Because she wants to share and receive information quickly.

Why #3: Why does she want to do that? Answer: To

know what's going on in the lives of her coworkers, friends, and family.

Why #4: Why does she need to know that? Answer: To know if someone needs her.

Why #5: Why would she care about that? Answer: She fears to be out of the loop."[2]

Julie's psychological triggers aside, we can probably all empathize with her actions. We all have our own reasons for why those notifications are important to us.

First, the notifications we receive seem simple, and the frequency of repetition breeds familiarity.

How many hundreds of times a day do you hear that ping or feel that vibration indicating another email, text message, social media post that needs your attention?

Those are small things, right? Little things are easy. Easy things fit in my secondary multitasking work queue!

Not so fast.

Recall that what we can't do well without shifting our attention, and paying the associated cost for doing so is taking on a second task that is mentally taxing.

Those notifications themselves might be small. The problem is they aren't tasks you can complete without pulling at least some of your focus away from your primary activity.

They are familiar, so we tell ourselves they are easy to process quickly. Is that actually true?

Even scanning and deleting newsletters and junk mail from your inbox requires some shift in focus, some allocation of attention, no matter how small.

The critical element we often overlook is that those notifications are representative of some form of communication.

Have you ever tried to follow two conversations at the same time? It doesn't often work out well.

You may take this beyond notifications and small, seemingly mindless tasks like email, and try to complete work with more substance.

Based on my own past behavior, I'll give you the benefit of the doubt. I'm going to assume you are only doing this when the competing task doesn't require much of your attention anyway. A meeting you probably should have declined, but chose to accept.

The problem is that when we show up, but don't actually *show up*, invariably someone will ask for our input. We are caught unprepared as our mind was elsewhere, focused on our secondary task.

What happens then? Both tasks are negatively impacted.

The meeting may get a previously unplanned follow up to deliver some critical piece of information that couldn't be produced on the spot.

The secondary task you worked on is still incomplete. Worse yet, you may have been able to finish the work, but it lacks your usual attention to detail, almost as if you were interrupted while working on it.

There is a problem with trying to multitask in these scenarios. Unlike the notifications and quick scans of email, we can't really justify to ourselves that the tasks don't need our full attention.

We know both tasks require our attention, but we convince ourselves that we can effectively slice up the time. That we can shift our focus quickly from one job to the other.

What this overlooks, however, is the context switch.

Context switching is a concept borrowed from computing. It describes how one component can work on different tasks if the necessary resources related to each task can be prepared and made available at the right time.

An easy way to relate it is to consider that we have a factory that produces widgets. Our widget business sells several different products, and each of those products is created by the same machinery and staff.

The catch is that each product requires different setup on the machines, and various source materials for the construction.

Let's assume that we deal with this by batching the work. Each day we run different shifts dedicated to producing the necessary volume of each widget that has been ordered, but there's some overhead involved.

Each time we have to change our production line to start building a different type of widget, we have to reconfigure the machinery. We also need to prepare all the source materials for the next production run.

Those efforts to reconfigure our factory are the context shift.

We lose productive time in our factory while we shift our resources from doing one thing to doing something else.

The same loss of productivity happens in our brain when we try to quickly move back and forth between the execution of two non-trivial tasks.

According to a 2012 article in Psychology Today, people who jump from one task to the next are up to 40% less productive and incur a cognitive penalty as well.[3]

So, in addition to losing small slices of time while your brain moves from one task to the other, you're also not doing your best work.

We give driving our full attention because we recognize the need to focus our attention, reaction, and motor skills entirely on the task at hand. While our work may not be life and death, as inattentive driving often is, doesn't it still deserve our full attention?

There are other benefits as well, aside from just the quality of work.

Consider the impact on your team or other coworkers. Whether we want to admit or not, our lower levels of attention are noticeable.

How often have you noticed someone you work with that's not quite engaged or fully connected to a conversation? They can see that in your behavior and performance as well.

So how can we break these habits, and solve these problems?

First, we need to realize that focus and prioritization will always produce our best work, in less time.

Your complete attention and focus for one hour are infinitely more valuable than half your attention spent on the same task for 30 minutes.

Take it a step further by challenging yourself to complete the tasks at hand faster, without compromising the quality of output. When you commit your full focus to one task, often, this is achievable.

Once you are committed to abandoning multitasking for good, there are some key actions you can take to help you along.

- Research and adopt a system of prioritization that works for you. Your goal here is to take a more intentional approach where we work on what matters — or as Stephen Covey said, "putting first things first."[4]
- We'll revisit this topic in a later chapter when we talk about taking back control of your time.
- Work from your prioritized list of established goals for each day. Use the list of goals to define

focused, dedicated work sessions where you commit to doing your best work for the time allotted.

- Take active steps to minimize distractions that would otherwise steal your focus. Separating yourself from your devices and liberal use of **Do Not Disturb** will help here.
- Decline meetings or events where your attendance adds no value or is not otherwise required. This will reduce pressure on you to work on other things during these meetings to "make up for the lost time." A pre-requisite to this will be that meeting invitations have a clear agenda. Don't hesitate to ask for one from the sender if it is not included.
- Block time in your schedule to deal with distractions (and the associated notifications) in chunks. Rather than allowing email to interrupt your focus, shut it down. Leave it for your next scheduled block of time where you can give *that* task your full focus and attention. We'll explore this particular step further in a later chapter.
- Encourage your peers, employees, and yes, even your manager to do the same. If you show up fully present and focused on the task or discussion at hand, it's reasonable to ask those around you to do the same.

FOCUSING ON ONE THING AT A TIME, TO THE BEST OF YOUR ability, will ensure you are bringing your full focus, creativity, and capability to every task or interaction.

As a leader, your commitment to focus extends beyond your behaviors and has a direct impact on your team. The example you set will influence their actions and that of others throughout the organization that you and your team interact with regularly.

Beyond leveraging consistent focus in your day to day work and interactions, you also must adopt a mindful approach to the challenges of leadership.

This will help you provide a more stable and focused environment for your team — one that leaves them free to focus as well.

The secret is that it is only two simple concepts.

Simple, in that, they are easy to understand — not always easy to adopt and practice as challenges arise.

First: Learn from the past but don't dwell on it.

Mistakes cannot be unmade, failures cannot be undone. At best, they can be *made right*. The one thing you can never do is reclaim lost time that was spent on destructive, negative behavior or backward-looking behavior.

I don't make this point to imply that accountability should be tossed out the window.

Ideally, you want to leverage your team's innate sense of responsibility to have a constructive conversation about improving after a critical failure. Stay focused on useful changes rather than assigning fault.

When you have a team staffed with high-performing professionals that take pride in their work, focusing on fault, highlighting failure too much will drive them away.

Keep any analysis of failure constructive, a forward-looking learning experience — don't dwell on the adverse outcomes.

Second: plan for the future, don't fixate on it.

Just as negative attention on the past can have undesirable effects with your team, time spent thinking about and planning for the future must also be carefully considered.

No one can fault planning, it makes good sense in business and in life. Of course, the phrase "analysis paralysis" is common for a reason.

Don't let your fear of failure or aversion to risk force you into a practice of never taking a step forward because your plan is incomplete or not quite ready.

Commit to learning from any mistake you make. Avoid making a mistake a second time. If it happens a second time, avoid making it a third. A fourth time? Well, at that point, maybe you need to revisit your approach to learning — but you get the idea.

As leaders, we absorb risk for our team.

That's what being the decision-maker means: sometimes, you won't have all the answers. You may not be able to get all of the ideal inputs necessary to make a fully informed decision.

Weigh the risks, take responsibility, and move ahead.

You might fail, but if you do nothing at all, failure becomes a certainty.

To be a truly effective leader, you must take control of your time and energy. You must do this not only for yourself but for your team. Learning to be more focused and present as a regular practice will help you achieve this.

This is a crucial lesson that the remainder of the book will build upon.

———

Leaders Take Action

- *List all the ways you can think of that you inadvertently (or intentionally) subject yourself to a context switch.*
- *Brainstorm 5 ways you can avoid context shifting, that can be implemented immediately.*
- *What are the things you do that cause you to be less than present for your team?*
- *For each item above, identify a solution or change that will avoid distracting behavior.*

7

LEADERS MANAGE COMMUNICATION

Communication is a core skill that we all must develop if we want to succeed in our professional lives. Being a leader requires that you raise your communication skills to an entirely new level of mastery.

It is no longer sufficient that you possess well-honed communication skills of your own. You have to assume the extra responsibility of managing the general state and flow of communication on your team.

What do I mean by state and flow? Let's come back to that in a minute.

I'm only going to touch briefly on essential communication skills in this book. You've hopefully developed your own ability to effectively communicate as you worked your way to a management role.

As an individual, you can express what you need, what you want, and what you think on a particular topic. You are comfortable, or at least capable, with providing direction, instruction, and opinions in a group or individual setting.

Back to Basics

If you feel like you need more work on your base skills, I've included some links to a few useful articles in the references for this chapter. These should get you started on the key areas you need to consider, and you can expand your learning from there.[12]

If you've put reviewing the communication basics out of mind, thinking to yourself, "Nah, I've got this. I'm a great communicator!" Maybe you should give them a read anyway. There's always room for improvement. If not in your own skills, in your ability to better observe and understand the people around you.

State and Flow

Review completed, mastery achieved?

Great! We are going to approach this topic from a less conventional angle than you may be used to, and I want you to be prepared.

What exactly do I mean by managing the state and flow of communication on your team?

Let's visualize your team as a body of water. I'm originally from the high desert region of Oregon, so picture a pristine mountain lake. The water is calm, clear, and clean. It's also generally cold, so I don't recommend an early spring swim.

This pristine state is the ideal state of communication on your team.

Calm, clear, clean.

Calm, so the team can express their thoughts about the group, or the work being done, without fear of reprisal. Emotions are present, we're all human after all, but they provide the passion and inspiration that energizes the team and keeps them engaged and excited about their work.

Clear, in that the team has established and normalized patterns of communication that ensure everyone can be well understood. The group adopts standard terms and language that evolves over time. There is an understanding that confusion on a topic needs to be addressed, questioned, and clarified.

Clean, in that there are no negative topics or patterns of communication that the team avoids. Problem areas that lead to a downward spiral of negativity that impacts the whole team, and are thus avoided instead of being addressed — like polluted water.

That brings us to the flow of communication. Our mountain lake is fed by streams, rainfall, and snow runoff. Other outlets and evaporation form the complete circle that defines the flow of water in and out of the lake. The water flows naturally unless something external is done to impact that process.

Communication on our team also needs to flow naturally. There should not be any unnatural impediments to the flow. This includes communication between members of the group, and with people external to the team. I don't use flow in this sense to mean transparency. While a policy governing transparent and acceptable sharing of information is necessary, the focus here is on the channels of communication. The ability to communicate openly and effectively with anyone.

To achieve a healthy state and flow of communication on our team, we will be exploring how our team communicates based on their personalities.

We'll also explore a critical indicator that even expert

communication skills won't help with if you don't manage it carefully: stress.

Introverts and Extroverts

Understanding introvert and extrovert personalities and how they communicate is a skill you will need to master to lead your team effectively.

Introversion and extroversion are extreme opposite states that exist on a spectrum, as defined by Carl Jung in his theory of *Psychological Types*.[3]

I've broken down the key points for each personality type below into independent categories, but, as you can probably attest, people are not so easily classified.

People usually exhibit a blend of traits from the two categories, rather than being strictly aligned to one or the other.

I'm an introvert, through and through. Even so, I can, at times, exhibit behaviors or take actions that make me seem more extroverted.

Public speaking is a great example.

Few things make me more uncomfortable than speaking to a large group of people. And of course, in true introvert style, I would define "large" as any group containing more than three people.

I do it anyway.

Why? Why do something that feels so against my nature, out of my comfort zone?

I do it because it is the most effective way to lead at that particular moment. It's necessary, and my commitment to leading supersedes my discomfort.

I make this point only to reinforce the need to avoid

categorizing everyone you interact with at one extreme or the other.

We humans are complicated.

Introverts

Introverts are generally considered to be more inwardly focused. Their own thoughts, feelings, or current mood impact their behaviors and reactions more than any external source.

As a result, more introverted people tend to be quieter in nature. They will often appear reserved and be slower to interact in group settings.

A common way to evaluate someone's tendency toward introversion is to consider how they respond to events that require a lot of interaction with a larger group of people. If such activities are tiring, require a lot of energy, and leave you feeling drained, you may have a more introverted nature.

As you start to establish a strategy for how you will manage the communication needs of the introverted personalities on your team, consider the communication needs of the more introverted members.

Introverts are less outspoken, but this doesn't mean they don't have anything to say. You will need to manage the team interactions carefully and ensure there is space for their contributions. As the extroverted types in the room will generally tend to fill the spaces with talk, the introverts can be frustrated by the need to interrupt or talk over others to be heard. This is difficult for them, and often they will opt just to withhold any input to the discussion.

. . .

INTRODUCTS MAY BE MORE COMFORTABLE SHARING THEIR INPUT in one to one settings. Allow for this, but recognize that there may be a need to strike a balance between accommodating individual interactions and allowing them to share essential insights in a group setting. Their desire for recognition in a group setting will vary — some introverts hate it; others prefer occasional group attention.

Extroverts

Extroverts are more outwardly focused. This doesn't presume that their own thoughts or feelings are disregarded, or have less impact than they would an introverted person. For an extrovert, those thoughts and emotions need to be expressed externally. Where introverts need to process their thoughts internally, extroverts prefer sharing ideas and exploring their meaning as they see how they are received by others.

Extroverts are often the "life of the party," outgoing, vocal and energetic. Let's use the large group event as a measure again. If interacting in social scenarios leaves you feeling energized, and the thought of time spent alone is more draining or undesirable, you may have a more extroverted nature.

The extroverted personalities on your team may initially seem to need less attention from you to facilitate successful communication. As outspoken and comfortable as the extroverts are in a group setting, they don't need any guidance, right?

This is a common misconception, and you should adapt your strategy appropriately to ensure you are meeting the needs of the team's extroverts.

Extroverts are more outspoken, but we must recognize

that the way that extroverts use verbal communication can be quite different from their introverted counterparts. Introverts often lean toward not voicing an opinion or thought until it is fully formed. It is considered internally, and then a decision is made to express it to the group. Extroverts conversely will vocalize both to communicate and to explore concepts they are working through. As you balance the personalities on your team, be careful not to stifle the exploratory conversation from the extroverts in favor of making space for the introverts. The extroverted types need this dialog to occur.

Extroverts generally need recognition and acknowledgment of their contributions to happen in the group environment. I'm not referring to praise or accolades, though those things are essential. What we need to realize is that the extroverted team members may present a confident appearance as they communicate an idea, but they often still expect to be challenged. Encourage an environment, starting first with your own actions and behaviors, where this necessary questioning and challenging of the extroverts can occur. This is another area the introverts may find difficult, just as the extroverts may struggle with leaving some air space for the introverts to step into.

Finding Balance

You are probably starting to realize that maintaining the natural function of the pristine mountain lake of communication is going to be quite a challenge.

As I said, we humans are complicated.

The key to successfully achieving this is going to be a repeated concept throughout this book. You should not be shouldering this responsibility alone.

You need to lead this effort, not pull it step by agonizing step alone. Your goal here is to establish a goal for the team that focuses on everyone taking appropriate measures to recognize the needs of the group as a whole and compromise to achieve that balance.

Balance the group interactions in a way that serves both personality types and creates an environment where they can thrive as a team is difficult. You must recognize that the more group interactions that are required, the more draining it will be for the introverted personalities.

Conversely, the extroverts need an open environment where dialog can flow freely to advance ideas and keep them energized and excited about the work the team is doing.

The Stress Gauge

You've probably seen the temperature gauges in cars, right? There's usually one to measure the oil temperature and another for the radiator.

We learned some critical things in the long process of developing a modern vehicle. Observation and experimentation have taught us that heat exposure over long periods is bad for the engine.

I have experienced this first hand recently as the radiator in my car decided it had enough and just stopped working as well as it should. There were many warning signs. The fan was behaving oddly, running long after the car was shut down, and it was noticeably louder than usual. The temperature gauge was periodically creeping higher and higher. Finally, the over-temperature warnings in the car started appearing, sounding the final alarm that immediate attention was needed.

I was observant enough of the change in behavior that I was able to drive the car to the shop and get it repaired. Aside from the pain of the repair bill, this scenario could have been much worse. Had I ignored the warnings, eventually, the radiator would have shut down completely, leaving the car a very decorative piece of furniture in my garage.

You have access to a similar warning gauge as you monitor communications within your team. That gauge is "The Stress Gauge".

Just as any excess temperature may cause several breakdowns in your vehicle, uncontrolled levels of stress can cause equally catastrophic disruptions with your team.

Consider the cost of emotional or highly stressful interactions over the long term.

I use the term cost intentionally.

We pay for highly charged emotional incidents by an increase in the general stress level of our team.

We also pay for suppression of the events that lead to these types of incidents, as the underlying problems don't go away if they are left untended.

Stress will kill your ability to lead.

Stress will destroy your relationships with your team and other colleagues, and left unchecked, it can bleed into your relationship with your family.

Unmanaged stress will turn you into the worst version of yourself.

These same outcomes and effects of stress apply equally to everyone on your team. While we will each react to stress in different ways, we are all affected by it, without exception.

If you've successfully created a cohesive unit, where your team is connected and supportive of each other, you'll find the effect of stress is minimized. The team that supports each other and absorbs and mitigates stressful situations together will perform better over the long term.

Left unchecked and unmanaged, however, even the best team will succumb to stress. The groups' ability to handle stress will be higher, but it still has an upper limit.

Like temperature, stress is an indicator that there is something wrong. If your team is resourced appropriately, working together well, and developing effective processes and procedures, the work that needs to be done should be manageable.

The state and flow of your team's communication, if developed well, provides you the necessary gauge where stress will appear, and ideally be addressed and removed.

Discussing the stresses the team shares, as well as those that manifest individually, will ensure your team continues performing at peak levels, well into the future.

Effective communication as a leader requires a level of awareness and mastery that is not often seen or needed in an individual contributor. You can no longer focus only on developing an ability to communicate that enables you to be independently successful. You have to build the skills necessary to manage the state of communication on your team as a critical sub-system that warrants constant monitoring.

The skills and systems we develop in the remainder of the book will help you achieve this.

———

Leaders Take Action

- *Identify three areas where you feel you could improve as a communicator.*

- *For each of the areas listed above, identify one or more ways you can address your weaknesses. (Books, courses or training, guided practice, coaching, etc.)*
- *What are some areas that need improvement within your team's ability to communicate?*
- *For each of the areas listed above, again, identify one or more ways you can address the problem. (Books, courses or training, guided practice, coaching, etc.)*

8

LEADERS TAKE CONTROL OF THEIR TIME

How often have you complained there is not enough time in the day?

Do you find yourself faced with yet another full day of meetings? What about a never-ending task list that is woefully short on completed check marks?

How does that generally make you feel about your work? Your job? Your day or your week?

Let's make it multiple choice:

(a) stressed out,

(b) overwhelmed, or

(c) exhausted.

On the worst days, it's probably the hidden answer:

(d) all of the above.

Stress is insidious.

Most people don't have a high tolerance for operating at a heightened stress level, yet others seem to thrive on it.

Are they just some kind of hyper-performing robots masquerading as people until they overthrow humanity?

Unlikely, the reality is everyone reacts to varying levels

of stress in different ways. It's as much about our personalities as our personal behaviors.

Now, you might be thinking to yourself:

"I eat stress for breakfast, it's the secret to my awesomeness. Are you saying I might be a sleeper agent for the robot overlords?"

I'm not ruling it out. After all, I don't really know you.

Joking aside, what I've found to be true for the people I've worked with that are high performers is much simpler.

The answer is not that these ultra achievers have an advanced skill set that you don't possess.

They also don't have access to more time than you do. We all have the same 1,440 minutes per day.

Their apparent high tolerance for stress is a function of the systems they've developed to manage their time and other available resources.

I say apparent tolerance for stress because the ultimate effect of putting these systems in place is that you accomplish more *without incurring the same level of stress*.

Indeed, even the high-performers around us have their limits. They've simply developed systems for working that place their limits much higher than those around them.

In the previous chapter, we discussed the need to set aside the belief that to get more done, we need to do more concurrently. There are productivity gains to be had by improving the level of focus we give to each task.

In this chapter, we will go a step further to specific techniques to manage and control your time.

Step 1: The Time Inventory

Learning to manage time more effectively requires that you first gain an understanding of how you spend your time currently.

If we don't know where we are, successfully planning how we will get to another destination is difficult.

We will start by recording an inventory of your day to day time.

What do I mean by an inventory of time?

Simple: record how you spend your day, and try to be as accurate as possible, but don't go overboard. It's perfectly fine if you round to 15-minute blocks. If your inventory is measured to the second, you've overdone it.

If you've never attempted this, or you are struggling with how to approach the task, use your calendar. If you have an email, you have access to a digital calendar. And, who doesn't have access to email?

If you don't want to use an existing calendar for this exercise, set up a new calendar using a free service. Google Calendar[1] is a natural choice.

Start by adding blocks of time to your calendar for every significant activity in your day.

What do I mean by blocks of time? Add meetings with no attendees.

Update those blocks as the time spent on the represented task changes or even moves around.

The level of detail is not overly significant, just leave yourself a quick note in the description to remind you how the time was spent.

At the end of the week, group all the items you recorded into logical categories and sum the time spent for each.

As an example, you might end up with something that looks like this:

- Internal Meetings: 18 hours
- External Meetings: 8 hours
- Project work: 4 hours

- Email & Office Time: 6 hours
- Other: 4 hours

The concept of **Office Time** is something I find useful. I use it to collect the time spent updating my calendar, dealing with emails, and other administrative tasks that need time but don't fit elsewhere.

Did you find anything surprising in how you spend your time?

Without exception, every person I've guided through this exercise has been surprised by how the numbers add up in at least one category.

Step 2: Managing Focus Interrupts

Now that you have a working process in place to pay closer attention to how you spend your time, let's push it a step further.

I've written previously about the effect of focus (or lack of focus) on the quality of our work. In this step, we're going to start paying close attention to this particular problem.

I want you to keep a notebook or scratchpad handy throughout the day. As you are engaged in any particular work session or activity, record on the paper when you are interrupted in any way.

For each interruption, add one or two words, so you know what caused it, and approximately how long you spent on the detour activity.

Did you stop to respond to an email notification? Email, 10 minutes.

Did you take an unplanned phone call? Phone call 15 minutes.

Mark it all down.

We don't need to overcomplicate this. In fact, we need to ensure that we don't let this activity itself become an interruption. For that reason, I recommend paper over a digital solution, though you are, of course, free to do whatever makes you most comfortable.

Here's the challenging part.

I also want you to recognize when you are distracting yourself. When does your focus fade? When does your mind wander? How many times when you are scheduled to be working on a large project do you end up checking social media quickly and lose track of 20 minutes?

Record every occurrence that you recognize, and try to be more mindful about when this happens. Be honest with yourself here, it can be enlightening.

In your gap between activities throughout the day, or at the end of the day, take your log of interruptions and record it in the calendar event that represents the activity time you just finished.

At the end of the week, categorize the interruptions just as you did the activity types in the last step. Add all of it to your time inventory.

As an example, your interruptions might look something like this:

- Email: 2 hours
- Phone: 1 hour
- Distracted/Focus: 2 hours

This addition to our time inventory provides us some interesting insights. You will start to understand not just how you spend time on the items captured, but how those items are actually impacting the focused work you recorded earlier.

Step 3: Prioritize Your Work

Once you understand where your time is spent, it's time to adopt a practice of ruthless prioritization.

I want you to question the importance of every task you undertake. Our purpose every day is not to be busy, but to be productive. We do this by being more intentional about how we spend our time, and to achieve that, we have to understand the priority of tasks we are responsible for.

There are many ways to approach prioritization. I'm going to share my favorite: the prioritization matrix. If you have a system you like, or this isn't a good fit for you, then feel free to adopt something else.

Be ruthless and honest in your prioritization.

Try to avoid assigning priority to something based on personal feelings like whether or not you enjoy the task. It's common and natural to want to procrastinate the items that we don't enjoy doing anyway, but that doesn't help us become more productive.

Consider external factors such as deadlines or dependencies with other people or teams.

Not everything is a high priority. If you struggle with this, approach the prioritization assignment as a budget. If you think both items rate the highest priority, assume you can only pick one. Give the other task a lower rating.

The prioritization matrix takes these into account naturally. To use the prioritization matrix, you rank all your tasks on two spectrums: Urgency and Importance.

If we draw a 4x4 grid with urgency tracked on the vertical, and importance tracked on the horizontal, all our tasks will fall into one quadrant or category:

- Not Urgent/Not Important (lower-left)

- Urgent/Not Important (upper-left)
- Urgent/Important (upper-right)
- Not Urgent/Important (lower-right)

Urgent items would be those tasks with a deadline assigned or where an external person, team, or customer has a dependency on your work. Non-urgent items have no particular time requirements, but just need to be done — maybe.

Importance is a determination of how critical the task is. Important items are required, and not possible to remove from your task list. Non-important things are the opposite: they are less significant, possibly even something you can skip entirely.

Now you have a prioritized task list. You can choose work that is both urgent and important first, moving on to the lower-ranked items as you have available time.

Whatever system you choose, it should not produce a list that is completely lacking in judgment. You still select what you will work on, but the system you adopt should provide a framework to make the decision process more manageable.

Step 4: Saying No

You are being more intentional about how you spend your time.

You are treating that time like the valuable commodity it is.

You may, however, still find some things just don't fit.

You made a legitimate effort to ensure that every task on your list isn't the highest priority, and yet the list of top priority items is still extensive.

There really is not enough time in the day.

There is a solution to this, and you've done the work to understand where your time is spent, so you have the data necessary to take the next step.

I want you to get comfortable with and embrace the power of **saying no.**

Let's consider a concept that I'm going to borrow from economics. Opportunity Cost[2] is the loss of potential gain from other alternatives when one alternative is chosen.

By saying yes to everything, what critical tasks are you failing to complete? What is the cost to you or your team when those tasks are not taken up?

Say no, but do so knowing that you understand precisely what your capacity is, and the value and relative importance of the task you are refusing.

Say no strategically. Then carry on with your day.

Now that you are comfortable with saying no to things, you've got more flexibility in how you act on the items populating the prioritized list.

- Do the work
- Do the work, later
- Delegate the work
- Say no, and delete that from your list

This flexibility to action your tasks in the most appropriate way for each item and considering your current competing requirements is vital. It allows you to get your own day under control. Deferring or deleting the things that aren't a good use of your time or delegating appropriate items out to your team frees you to focus on what is most important.

We'll return to the topic of delegation in Part III of the book.

Step 5: Saying Maybe or "I reserve the right to say no later."

As a final step, we're going to continue building on this iterative approach to intentional time and task management.

You now have a functional and accurate accounting of time on your calendar. You are comfortable with saying no to protect your ability to do your best work on things that matter.

We have one last skill to adopt.

We're going to give ourselves the ability to say maybe when a no would be an inappropriate response. One that is too strong given the audience, or where we simply can't decide with the information we have.

We'll rely on our handy calendar for this change, as well. Start by responding as tentative where you don't feel comfortable sending an outright decline to a request.

Now, at a regular interval, I want you to start reviewing your schedule. Do this weekly if you can.

When you conduct this review, give particular attention to the tentative items on your calendar. After a few days, how do you feel about that event? Have you gotten more comfortable with saying no?

Good, decline it.

If a second look or more information you've received in the interim convince you it's worth your time, send an acceptance.

What should your criteria be for accepting or declining a meeting?

If a meeting doesn't have an agenda: decline it with a note explaining why.

As new meetings come in, if you can't justify your attendance against your other priorities: decline it.

If you aren't sure, reply as tentative — say maybe. Review it in a few days, and if you still can't see the value: decline it.

In this way, we continue to evolve the time and task management skills we've adopted by recognizing that sometimes we can't make a firm decision on the spot. This gives us some necessary flexibility without sacrificing the benefits of our new system.

There will always be more things to get done, another task to complete, another meeting you could take.

With the right system, you will be the next high-performer that your colleagues look to and say, "How do they get so much done?"

As a leader, you must become more intentional about how you spend your time and encourage your team to do the same. Stop accepting every meeting without evaluation or thought. Gauge the importance, prioritize, consider whether it can and should be delegated, and, most importantly, recognize the value of your time and spend it accordingly.

———

Leaders Take Action

- *Complete the time inventory and review the results. What did you learn that was surprising or unexpected?*

- *Have you adopted a strategy for prioritizing your work?*
- *Have you extended your vocabulary for responding to requests beyond saying 'YES' to everyone? If not, when will you start?*

9

___

LEADERS BUILD INFLUENCE

There are many paths to leadership.

You may be promoted to a position where you are the line manager for one other person. You might have taken a much more significant role leading a division or department, with a multi-tiered management structure reporting to you. You may have assumed management of a team somewhere between those two extremes.

Congratulations, each of you in those roles is now a leader.

You may not manage a team of employees directly but instead manage the work done by contractors, virtual assistances, or other external partners and vendors.

You are a leader, as well.

What if you don't manage any people, either externally or internally? What if your area of responsibility is a product, project, or another *thing*?

Yes, Product Managers, Project Managers, Event Coordinators, you are all leaders too.

If you've held one or more of the above positions, you

may be saying, "These roles are nothing alike." And, you'd be right.

Each of these roles has a very different grant of authority. They each may carry a very different title. In some cases, you may not feel like, or be recognized as a Person In Charge.

You might be in a role where you are absolutely intended to be in charge, and yet some days will still feel completely out of control.

How can these roles that are so different all be categorized as leadership positions then? How can you avoid being in charge in name only?

Authority, right? You are in charge or have a responsibility that requires you to manage something or someone, so you must have the authority to command the resources you need to be successful.

Not exactly.

Management or leadership built on authority is what is commonly referred to as the "command and control" model. It has its place.

An obvious example is in the military. Following orders is kind of a big deal.

Even in that highly regulated environment, however, authority alone is not the only driver of successful leadership. In the business world, the shift away from a pure authority-based leadership style is even more pronounced.

Don't get me wrong, some of these positions will still require you to assume the authority necessary to execute the job at hand successfully. But power isn't helpful for the product manager that needs to collaborate across many different departments to successfully deliver her product.

We need a more versatile, more nuanced approach to leadership.

We need to recognize and cultivate a set of skills that work together. Skills that will both position us as a leader, and provide a reliable means of control that is viable for the long term.

Influence is the key.

It is influence, not authority alone that provides the definitive measure of our ability to lead over the long term, and in any situation.

Even in traditional command and control environments, influence is heavily utilized, if you know what you are looking for. Call it camaraderie, esprit de corps, brother/sisterhood. The authority model that is so obvious is overlaid by practices that enable and build influence within the unit.

The traditional salute exchanged between officers and enlisted is a prime example. It is a distinctly recognizable sign of authority *and* respect. This is not to say that every enlisted person respects every officer they salute. A reasoned argument can be made, however, that the most successful officers lead via a carefully cultivated balance of authority and influence within their unit.

Regardless of how you arrive at a leadership role, your effectiveness as a leader will be dependent on your ability to build and maintain influence with the people around you.

When all you have is a hammer, every problem looks like a nail. [1]

Let's make sure your toolbox has more in it than just the hammer of authority.

What do you mean by influence, exactly?

You've probably guessed by now that when I refer to influence, I'm not suggesting that you build up an Instagram following or start a new channel on YouTube.

The dictionary definition is simply: the capacity to have an effect on the character, development, or behavior of someone or something, or the effect itself. [2]

Now we're getting somewhere. Changing behaviors definitely sounds like a useful capability if we want to have some control over the outcomes of our team or the efforts made by the people around us.

Effecting character and development sounds promising, as well.

Have you ever received advice or guidance from someone that you adopted? A coach, mentor, family member, or friend, perhaps? That person influenced you to make what was, hopefully, a positive change.

That person influenced you to get the desired result by affecting a change in your behavior, character, actions, or growth.

This is the skill we need to adopt as leaders.

We must cultivate the ability to influence others towards a positive outcome that helps us meet our responsibilities and the responsibilities and expectations of our team.

So, how do we build influence?

Socrates said, "I know nothing except the fact of my ignorance." [3]

Clearly, he was talking about relationships. What else could it be?

People are complicated, and what works for you with one person may or may not work for you with another. You can and will find people where you can't form a working connection, much less develop any noticeable influence.

I've found the things that feel natural to me through trial and error.

Many, many errors.

Eventually, I learned how to be myself, but still build a stronger relationship with the people around me by understanding a bit more about each of them.

You see, influence is not a finite state. A thing to be achieved. It is a measurement, the quantitative expression of your capability to induce a change in another person.

It's an indicator of the quality of the relationship between two people. Now you are probably starting to understand why there is no simple set of instructions.

People are complicated, and our relationships with people reflect that complexity.

While there are no specific practices that work for everyone, I can provide a few guiding principles. These principles will help you discover the methods that work best for you.

Principle #1: Trust

Influence is built on trust, and trust must be mutual.

Consider what the ultimate effect is when someone, either consciously or unconsciously, allows you to influence them. That person is relinquishing some of their own control. Just enough to say, "When you talk, I'm willing to listen and really consider what you have to say."

They are voluntarily giving you a limited ability to exert control over the way they think, behave, and act.

These are not things that we relinquish to others lightly, and never voluntarily to someone who we don't trust.

So, your first guiding principle is to build a strong foundation of trust in all of your relationships.

Start by trusting others.

If you struggle with extending that trust to others, don't be surprised if they find it difficult to trust you in turn.

People may not be able to articulate their reasons. It may be our innate survival mechanisms kicking in. We just sense something is off, and our guard goes up.

Be authentic in word and deed.

If you fall into the trap of saying things because you feel they are what you should say, but you don't believe them yourself, your actions will tell. Speak honestly and openly with everyone. Then follow-through. Ensure your actions match your words.

Meet your obligations.

Do the things you say you will do. If you commit to something, hold yourself accountable. When you fail, own that failure, apologize, and do better next time. Don't promise to do better next time. *Do better next time.*

Be transparent when possible, and honest always.

In business, as in life, there are times when you must range from cautious where, when, and how you share information. It doesn't require a security clearance to realize that it is not always prudent, or sometimes even legally permissible, to share everything. The further you advance in your career, the more this prudence becomes necessary, as the impact and importance of the information you acquire will continue to grow.

Share information with those around you, when it is prudent and justified to do so, and be honest about the prevailing situation when it is not.

Secrets are the seed that destroys trust. Don't believe me? Watch any episode of any soap opera, from any decade, since the advent of the television. Someone has a secret. Someone else will find out. There will be drama and tears.

Trust others. Be trustworthy in return. Be decent, which leads us to our next principle.

Principle #2: Respect

Influence is built on respect, and like trust, it must be mutual.

Obviously, you can't make someone respect you. We only have complete control over ourselves, so let's start there.

As we focus on being intentional in our respect for others, so too will they respect us.

Let's explore some common sense advice that is unfortunately not always commonly observed.

Be self-confident.

No, I'm not advising you to *fake it until you make it*. Recognize your own skills, be confident in your own abilities, and let that confidence tastefully manifest in your personality. If, by your actions and mannerisms, you show people that you are not confident in yourself, why should they have any confidence in you either?

Be humble.

Don't let your self-confidence cross a line into an excessive expression of ego. Accept praise for a job well done graciously, then share it liberally with those people around you that are deserving.

Ask for help or advice.

Once you've committed to being humble, you're now able to ask for help. Your ego has gotten out of the way. If you need help, there is no more natural way to show your respect for someone else then to ask for their advice or assistance. In addition to solving your own immediate need, you are doing so in a way that says, "I respect and value opinion."

Listen.

Don't navigate every conversation, merely waiting for

your opportunity to talk. Listen to people, and show them you respect them and want to *hear* what they have to say.

Be patient with others.

No one is perfect. Every one of us, at times, needs time and space to work through something. A concept we are struggling with. A situation we weren't prepared for. Life. We're all human. We make mistakes. Give people the space they need to move forward, and where appropriate a hand up.

Treat everyone with respect.

Some people will tell you, "Respect is earned." I would argue that influence is earned. Trust is earned. Respect can and should be given because how you treat people says more about you than it does about them.

Be organized and punctual.

While this is good advice that will serve you well in every aspect of your life, it's particularly crucial in your professional relationships. We are all struggling to do more with less time — it's the primary theme of this book — and the least we can do for each other is to respect our time. Show up, on time, prepared to bring your best to the task or conversation at hand.

Be good at your job.

Put in the effort required to *excel* at what you do. The people around you don't need to fully understand your area of excellence to appreciate the work you did to achieve it — and they will respect that.

Share your expertise, but be open about your limitations.

Know what you don't know!

When you are a highly-skilled expert in a particular area, people will recognize when you freely share the knowledge you've worked so hard to acquire. Conversely, you also have an opportunity to bolster their opinion of you when you are open and honest about your weaknesses or gaps in skill or knowledge.

Recognize and respect people's boundaries.

We all need different things from every relationship, whether personal or professional. That includes where we place our boundaries. Sometimes people will need extra space to keep a separation between the segments of their lives. Others may need less space, more connection. There is a balance to be struck with each person, and you have your own boundaries as well.

Care about the people around you.

If you want people to respect you, show them you care. Respect their boundaries, and be yourself, but find ways to authentically show the people around you that they are more than just cogs in a machine, a resource to be leveraged. Show them that they are valuable people first, and useful employees or team members second.

Again, be decent.

Influence, like authority, if abused, will be lost.

Authority may provide a means to an end, and it has its place as a tool for every flexible and effective leader. But the investment in developing influence and key relationships with the people around you will enable you to lead your team consistently and effectively through a much broader range of challenges and achievements.

Do this well, and you are not just leading your team but setting an example for your entire organization that embodies the culture and practice of transformational results-oriented leadership.

———

Leaders Take Action

- *Consider your team and objective responsibilities. Is a command and control, or more traditional authority-based leadership model more common? If so, how can you work towards an influence based approach?*
- *On a scale of 1-10, 1 being the lowest, rate your influence with your team.*
- *Now, brainstorm at least 5 ideas that you could use to build and improve your influence with the team.*
- *Plan when and how you'll start executing the ideas you feel will be most effective. Don't be afraid to try something new!*

10

___

LEADERS CREATE SYSTEMS

D id you know that your decisions are actually made by your subconscious mind?

The work of Sigmund Freud has been studied for nearly a century. Even if you haven't studied psychology, you might still have picked up a passing understanding of how our minds work.

If not, let me catch you up just enough for our purpose in this chapter.

Freud proposed that your mind has three distinct functional areas: the conscious, the subconscious, and the unconscious. We're going to touch on an intriguing aspect of the relationship between the conscious and the subconscious.

The conscious mind provides the executive function: it is responsible for reasoning, direction, and communication, both internal and external. Your conscious mind decides where your focus should be, what work is most important to be executed.

The subconscious mind does the heavy lifting. Think of it as the worker function that does the job of locating, organizing, and surfacing information up to the conscious mind. The subconscious mind has full access to our memory and the unconscious portion of the brain. It draws on these as resources to meet the requests made by the conscious mind.

This includes decision making.

In a study published in 2008 in Nature Neuroscience, researchers monitored the brain activity of people asked to make a decision. In this case, the decision was to push a button with either their left or right hand. The participants were asked to indicate when they made their choice. What the researchers were monitoring, however, was the time just before the conscious decision.

What the researchers found is they could predict the decision the participants would make up to 7 seconds before the time the participant indicated they had made the decision. This was possible based on observations of brain activity several seconds before the time identified by the participant as the moment of choice.[1]

This shows that identifying a decision to be made is handled by the conscious mind, but the work of making that decision is handed off the subconscious. Once the decision is made, the resulting choice is then handed back up to our conscious mind to complete the loop.

Everything that we do can be understood as a series of decisions. You might consider them micro-decisions. We make the decision to move, or not, to keep walking, or not; thousands, if not millions of decisions every second.

And, the bulk of these decisions are not things that we actively think about doing. Our minds are processing inputs continuously from our senses. Making logical conclusions about how to act on that information and handing off the responsibility to see that it gets done to our subconscious.

How often do you think about walking? The physical

mechanics involved in walking from Point A to Point B. Unless you are one of those talented people that can fall up stairs and trip on nothing, probably not very often.

And yet, you can still walk across the room successfully.

What we overlook is that this is also a function of our subconscious mind. When we make the decision to walk across the room, we don't then consciously plot a course and think about each step. We leave that to our subconscious mind, that can handle those tasks quite well enough without our conscious brain micromanaging the process.

This dual-processing nature of our minds is not limited to mundane tasks like walking either. Any job or skill that you have practiced sufficiently that your brain has mastered the mechanics will be executed in the same way.

Think about when you first started driving. Remember how you felt, and the kind of attention and focus you applied. Now, think about what your focus looks like when you drive today.

Hopefully, as you got more comfortable with driving, you didn't drop your focus altogether. But, did you notice a distinct shift in how you mentally approach the activity when it was new to you, compared to how you approach it now?

When you first start driving, you probably made very conscious reminders to yourself to perform critical tasks. Check your mirrors. Don't forget to use your signals. Watch your blind spots. Always be scanning traffic.

I can remember running these things through my head. Almost as a mental checklist, trying to ensure I remembered all of the essential things I needed to be doing.

Do you think about those things now? I certainly don't. I still do them just as diligently as when driving was entirely new for me. Now, however, the processes seem automatic. I don't think about checking my mirrors, it happens naturally without directed thought. I'm thinking about the fact that I need to change lanes to be positioned for an upcoming turn.

My subconscious handles the organization and processing of the tasks necessary for me to successfully execute that higher-order decision. I signal, check my mirrors, and change lanes successfully. Based on an executive decision from my conscious mind that my next action that is a mile down the road and approaching fast.

So, what does this have to do with systems? Aren't we talking about systems in this chapter? And what does any of this have to do with leadership or managing a team?

This treatment of skills is not limited to walking, or driving, or any other everyday activities. The things that you have mastered in your professional life are treated no different by your mind. They are just another executive task that is worked in tandem by your conscious and subconscious mind.

Now, however, that mastery and seemingly automatic execution pose a different problem. It's challenging to recognize and describe something that we have entirely internalized.

This leads us to situations where we can complete a task with a level of mastery that we may not be able to explain adequately. Add the stress of deadlines, responsibilities, and expectations to that. Now we are at risk of falling into a trap where we have a team around us but find ourselves saying, "it's just easier if I do this myself."

We'll explore how and why we need to master delegation in Part III. First, we need a way to take what we know and share it effectively with our team.

To do that, we're going to explore a framework we can

use to discover the systems we have already developed and prepare to share them with our team.

The framework is simple. It only requires us to READ: Recognize, Evaluate, Adapt, and Describe.

R.E.A.D. on!

Recognize

Transitioning successfully into a leadership role requires us to become mentors, coaches, teachers. We have to learn to recognize how we do the things that we do well and how we can successfully teach them to others.

It's tough to teach things that we do more or less on auto-pilot. We don't think about the many steps involved in accomplishing something when we've mastered that task, and its execution comes naturally to us. Our subconscious just takes care of it.

We may not even recognize our own mastery in a particular area.

Consider time and task management systems, such as those we discussed in a previous chapter. I've had the opportunity to help several people struggling in this same area over the years, but I've never considered myself an expert on the topic of productivity.

These conversations about task management usually came about as a result of other unrelated discussions, where the problem of prioritizing and tracking work more effectively was mentioned in passing. I would offer a few suggestions that have worked for me, and often we would end up engaging in a full-blown discussion of the systems I use to manage work.

This always surprised me at first. The missing component for me was the recognition that I had established a level of expertise in addressing this problem that was immensely helpful to the other person.

I viewed the systems I was casually sharing as common knowledge: Hadn't everyone discovered a similar system of working already?

The mistake on my part was in marginalizing the years of practice and refinement that I'd spent developing those "simple" systems. I had cycled through many different approaches to the problem, some of which were complete failures. But that was not a recent occurrence for me. I've found systems that I like, that serve me well, and I've been using those systems successfully for years now. I never think about them, there is no need.

The problem arises when someone needs our guidance to solve the same problem. For skills that we've mastered — handing them off to be primarily managed by our subconscious — we often have the tendency to confuse that mastery with simplicity. We forget about the work we did to master that task, and look only at our ability to manage it with relative ease.

The natural conclusion then is that the task itself must not be difficult. Of course, this is incorrect. The task is no less complex than it was when we first encountered it. The skill we developed and systems we adopted have made the task *easy for us*, but if you remove those things, the inherent complexity remains the same.

This is our challenge in the first step of the framework. We must learn to identify where we have achieved a level of mastery that has enabled us to internalize a particular skill or skills.

Think about the things you do regularly in your current role (or a previous role, if it's more applicable to the people you need to lead).

Are you starting to list possible areas you can leverage your experience and skills into systems that would benefit your team or the people around you?

Great, let's move on to the second step of the framework.

Evaluate

As we reflect and identify each skill as a potential system, we also must ask: What purpose is the system meant to serve? What problem does it need to solve?

The purpose behind a particular system you've adopted may seem obvious to you, but this step is critical.

The systems you've adopted were developed to meet a particular need. When that need changes, often, the system must also change. Evaluating each system against its guiding principles helps you to understand better the choices that resulted in the system in its current state. Again, we're unpacking decisions that we likely made with the help of our subconscious. Since we're preparing to share this system with others, we need to be able to communicate not just what the system accomplishes, but why it was chosen or developed.

Remember that it's the conscious mind that's in charge of communication. We need to set it to work digging up the data from our subconscious that evolved this system, so we can then explain it to others.

After evaluating the system's purpose, you can then make an informed decision about whether this particular system is relevant, valuable, or appropriate for introduction to your team.

Understanding the intent behind a particular system prepares us to improve it, but it also prepares us to talk about it in a way that is easier to consume for the other person.

Continuing from the example above, when I introduced my own task management approaches to others, I began by explaining the purpose behind the system.

I could have taken an approach where I jumped immediately into teaching my exact steps for managing projects and tasks. But that would not have served them well. Their needs were not the same as mine. Some of the practices in the system would be confusing or distracting f they didn't have some insight into why those elements were necessary.

In this example, the project I was using as a backdrop for our conversations had frequently changing priorities coupled with minimal time allocated for project work. An essential requirement for me was to ensure that as priorities shifted, I could keep the focus on the long term vision. When time is a scarce resource, doing the wrong thing is more costly.

This led to a modification of the system I usually use for tracking project work that would combine the project vision, milestones, and tasks in one place. This forced me to evaluate each task added to the project to determine if it mapped directly to an intermediate goal and the project vision. Anything that didn't have a clear benefit needed to be deferred or deleted entirely.

Without explanation, these additional items would not have been apparent to those unfamiliar with it.

This is a simple example and probably seems logical at its surface. Ask yourself, though, how often do we jump immediately into describing for someone else *how* something is done, and skip right over *why* something is done?

Evaluating our systems will prepare us both to communicate the value of the systems we are sharing, as well as discuss and debate those systems with others.

That leads us to our next step in the framework: Adapt.

Adapt

Once we've determined that we have a proposed system that has clear value to our team, our next action is to identify areas where the system needs to change.

There are two essential drivers of change when you attempt to take an individual system and prepare to share it with a group.

First, you will need to identify any adjustments that need to be made to adapt the system to the skill sets of the people who will adopt it.

Just as you internalized the system and it's component skills as you mastered it, you've also internalized the improvements made over time.

As we progress through increasing stages of mastery in a given area, we continue to refine our skills. We keep learning. We adopt new practices that are more complex, but that our improved level of mastery allows us to complete with relative ease.

Consider how the systems you are preparing to share with your team will need to be adapted to their relative skill levels. Think about the progression they will naturally follow as their skills grow.

The second area of adaption is one of scale. The system you are evaluating and preparing to share with your team may have been developed as you were in an individual role.

How will that system need to change to be useful for your team? When you are evaluating methods for personal development, this is not really a concern. When the system is adopted by a group, however, it usually needs additional attention.

My own approach to task management recently had to evolve to address both of these concerns. The project in question has always been a solo effort, but another person joined the team. The new team member was less practiced with structured task management than I am. The system I was using at the time was also not well suited for use by a group of people.

In this case, I needed to adapt the system in several ways to onboard and enable the new team member. We moved to a different tracking platform. One that had better support for a shared team environment, and a lower barrier to entry to its use.

Think about the systems you want to introduce to your team, either as individuals or as a group. How will you need to adapt those systems to be effective?

Let's move on to the last step in the framework: **Describe.**

Describe

We've recognized an essential system or skill and evaluated its purpose against our current needs or the needs of our team. We've considered how we need to adapt that system to our team and their skill levels.

Now it's time for the final effort.

It's time to describe the system from start to finish. We'll deconstruct and detail the steps, skills, and resources necessary to successfully use the system.

I intentionally avoided the term **Document** here. If you've ever worked with software products, you probably recognize documentation as the job everyone loves to hate. I don't want you to get too hung up on how to describe your system. It may need formal documentation, it may exist only as tribal knowledge. It may be somewhere between the two extremes. I'll leave it to you determine what's most appropriate for your team.

Our goal is to ensure we have deconstructed the component skills and processes to consumable chunks that we can both communicate to others and facilitate the learning process.

We need to remove any inherent complexity that would discourage someone new to this system from getting started.

Remember that what we are proposing to the team may be something completely new. New things are often confusing, and we just don't know where to start to demystify them.

The strategy I recommend here is to break things down until they feel approachable and straightforward, or that they can't be broken down any further. The secret is that complicated things are really just a collection of simpler things that have been grouped together in an unfamiliar or unrecognizable way.

Big things are made of many small things.

Start by breaking down your system into sub-skills. Do this by identifying higher-order skills first, then break those skills down into progressively smaller sub-skills.

When skills are broken down into small enough pieces, they become like LEGO blocks. How many different things can you build with a box of LEGO bricks? The combinations are endless. The same is true of this inventory of skills. You and your team will consistently find new ways to take what you know and use it in new a context, or a new system.

Now that we an inventory of skills necessary to implement the system we are deconstructing, the next step is prioritization. Our goal here is to describe the system in a way that will help people learn and implement the system in as short a time as possible.

To do that, we can use a simple prioritization approach like the Pareto Principle (or the 80/20 rule). [2]

Review the deconstructed list of skills and order them by their value to the system. Now select the top 20% of skills with the highest value or impact on the operation of the system. These skills should represent approximately 80% of the skill mastery needed to implement the system effectively.

The prioritized list of skills can now be used to identify the key lessons or points of understanding necessary for successful execution. To do this, ask yourself: How did you learn this skill? How did you approach practicing it? What training or materials are available to assist or accelerate development?

As you identify ways to practice each skill, also consider what represents a useful measure of progress. How can you help someone learning this particular skill to evaluate their development and improvement? What does success look like?

Once progress in the skill is measurable, you can then establish an acceptable minimum skill level at which the ability can be used as a component of the system. Doing so ensures that you are defining a process that takes less time to get someone to a functional level, and then to continue improvement toward mastery.

Additionally, if you feel like your development has slowed, there is no better way to break out of that plateau than by teaching that topic to someone else.

Deconstructing and describing a system in this manner will help evolve your systems into a team setting. The introspection and focus on the depth of understanding necessary to teach that system to others will also raise your own skill mastery to new levels.

I used a similar framework to the one presented here to write this book. Over many years in various leadership roles, I internalized several systems that helped me become a successful leader, but articulating what those systems were was a challenge.

I had to step back and really consider what skills I rely on the most to lead my teams, and why those skills are essential. I then had to break those down further into their component parts to make them easier to explain, discuss, and apply.

Doing so has forced me to evolve my own approach to leadership and continue to grow my systems to meet new challenges.

The systems we create are like living things that evolve with each new person that adopts and improves them. That evolution can only happen if we take the time to recognize the value of those systems. Finally, we must describe those systems in a way that shows that value clearly, and be willing to embrace the change that comes with growth.

———

Leaders Take Action

- *Think about the objective responsibilities assigned to your team. Now, brainstorm at least 5 areas where introducing an evolving system would improve team performance.*
- *One of the key benefits of systems is the value they*

provide to new hires or changes in personnel. Well documented and understood systems reduce the onboarding time for each new team member. Considering the systems you identified above, or others that already exist, how can you improve each to facilitate knowledge transfer on your team better?

11

LEADERS OWN FAILURE AND SHARE SUCCESS

To transform yourself into an effective leader and prepare to delegate responsibility to your team, you first have some preparatory work to do.

How do you react when things go well? What about when things *don't* go so well? What is your relationship with praise or criticism?

Spend a few minutes looking inwards and considering these questions. They may seem a bit odd at first, and that's okay.

I'll share something unusual about me: Compliments embarrass me.

Admittedly, I don't really even understand why I find them embarrassing, but there it is.

Ironically, I appreciate recognition as much as the next person, and definitely notice when I feel like I've done something warranting some form of attention that is lacking.

And yet, if that recognition is complimentary, I'm still going to be embarrassed by it. It is, in fact, slightly embarrassing writing about how I have this weird reaction to complements that makes me feel embarrassed!

I share this with you here because it has a bearing on my own growth as a leader. You see, my embarrassment is not restricted to receiving compliments. Giving compliments to others makes me equally uncomfortable.

This is a problem for me as I want to build strong relationships with the people around me, and sometimes (even if it embarrasses us), we all need a compliment. We want to know that the work we're doing is both noticed and appreciated.

While I'm willing to consider that this personality quirk may be unique to me, it raises a point that we need to address together.

We all have our own personality quirks. As leaders, we need to turn our attention inward and really look closely at our relationship with and reaction to success and failure.

In this chapter, we're going to focus on how we effectively share ownership of success and failure by adopting a few critical behaviors. We're not going to dive deep into goal setting for success or how to mitigate risk and avoid failure, we'll get into that later.

In the next part of the book, we'll revisit both topics in more detail. For now, let's explore how we think about success and failure. How we behave when they occur, and how we may need to change as we step into a more leadership-focused role.

Letting Go

Leadership requires us to remain accountable while delegating responsibility for performance. It is a loss of direct control. This can, understandably, be an uncomfortable feeling.

In exchange for that loss of control, we gain the possibility of creating leverage and increased capability above and beyond what

we could achieve as individuals.

To do that, however, we have first to let go of something important. As an individual contributor, accountability and responsibility are inseparable friends. It's not common for them to be apart — they do everything together.

If you carry that expectation into your role as a leader, that friendship can quickly go downhill. Think of Thelma and Louise holding hands as they drive off of the cliff. It's a beautiful image of friends to the end, but I suspect you don't want your team to end in a fiery ball of death at the bottom of a cliff.[1]

At least, I hope not.

As you shift out of that individual contributor mindset, and move further into your role as a leader, get comfortable with letting go of direct responsibility.

We discussed trust in depth a few chapters earlier, and this is your first test of that commitment to extending trust to your team.

You are the person ultimately accountable for the output of your team. But you have to let go of the need to remain responsible for doing the work — and trust that your team can handle it.

Learning to Share

Once you have successfully let go of direct responsibility for everything that falls under your scope of accountability, you are ready to take the next step forward.

That step is something you probably learned in Kinder-garten: Sharing.

Specifically, I want you to share the results of success and failure. This behavior will be the first make or break moment that will test your trust in your team, and their faith in you.

For just a moment, imagine yourself back in the role of a team member. Individual contributor, accountable, and responsible.

You work hard to complete a task that was assigned to you, and the team is praised for successfully meeting its obligations. How would you feel if your manager were to take all the credit for that success?

Not happy, that's for sure. Definitely not increasing your feeling of trust with that manager.

What about when things don't go well? Maybe you finished your work, but it was a near miss, and some of the team weren't so lucky. Things fell through the cracks, and the team missed a key objective. The manager comes down hard on those with incomplete work. You finished your work, and you still get counseled on the need to be a better team player.

These are entirely fictional scenarios that if you've been in the workforce long enough, I'm sure you recognize that art really does imitate life.

How can you avoid these extremes of behavior, in a way that doesn't sacrifice your own ability to remain accountable for your personal objectives, and those of the team?

We need to share, but we need to strike an appropriate balance in how we do that.

Strive to be generous with praise, sharing the results of success liberally and frequently with your team. This builds trust with your team by clearly showing them that you trust them with essential tasks. It also indicates that you will ensure they are recognized for successfully meeting that responsibility.

When I ask you to share success by giving praise, I don't mean only by sharing positive responses with your team. I want you to commit to sharing the achievements of your team with *everyone*. You should be clear with your own manager how the group, and each individual, are working diligently to make the team successful.

You will want to find a balance that you are comfortable with, but I would challenge you to give away all of the praise. Keep none for yourself.

Why such an extreme position? Because it's impossible to achieve, but in the attempt at doing so, you will find the right balance. For me personally, doing this helps me to adjust to my compliment quirk. When I make a point to redirect *all of the praise* to my hard-working team, the most common response is a recognition of my leadership in making that success possible.

I can accept that compliment. I know at that moment that I've done everything I should have done to meet my responsibility to make my team successful. Not just as a unit with a mission within the organization, but as individuals as well.

What about failures? Should you share the negative things? How do you do that without breaking trust?

Yes, you need to share failures as well, but doing so requires a measured and considerate approach. You don't want to damage the trust you've built with the team, but you can't isolate them from failure completely.

In Part III, we're going to introduce the concept of learning from failure as a team and why you, as a leader, need to ensure this is a part of your team culture.

For now, I want you to focus on treating failure, precisely the opposite, as you treat success. This should be logical on its surface, failure, and success are opposites. It may also be quite uncomfortable, but the role of a leader is to retain accountability.

The buck stops here, as they say.

As you give away most, or ideally all of the responsibility for executing the team's work, your responsibility shifts. You shouldn't be building the widgets or making the sales calls, or troubleshooting issues on support tickets, or operating the machinery on the warehouse floor.

You do, however, retain sole responsibility for ensuring your team succeeds.

Entrepreneurs often talk about how they are balancing working *in* their business with working *on* their business. Treat your team just as you would if you were an entrepreneur running a business. Work on your team, not in it. And, this means attending to processes, resources, constraints, and all manner of other issues that lead to each failure.

This is another opportunity to build influence, respect, and trust with your team. When your team sees that you are taking responsibility for the environment that leads to any failure, and still holding them accountable for their performance, something interesting happens. They will recognize that you are creating an environment where they can succeed or fail based on their efforts while someone attends to the coordination and, well, leadership.

Embrace the Hive Mind

You may struggle to adjust your behaviors around success

and failure, and let go of responsibility. Forming new habits isn't easy, and these are no exception.

As we close out this chapter, I want to provide you with a deceptively small change in how you speak to the team. This change can help you reinforce the behaviors above, and the relationship you are working to build with your team.

I'm not what you would call a die-hard Sci-Fi fan. I have, however, read and watched enough of the genre to have seen a common theme emerge.

In any Sci-fi adventure where we have our heroes facing off against an alien insect-like race, there is usually some concept of a hive mind. It doubles as a repository of knowledge and means of communication.

Whenever we're exposed to some translation of the language, one thing stands out: The bugs don't think or speak in terms of the individual.

They say "we" and "us," not "you" and "I."

Say what you want about bugs, I don't care for them myself, but they are on to something here.

As the team's leader, you have a responsibility to shape the team into a highly functional unit. Building trust, respect, and influence built on a shared understanding and treatment of success and failure will take you a long way.

Sometimes, however, it's the little things that really work to reinforce our more significant behaviors. Little things like the choice of language that we use when speaking to and about the team.

Speaking in terms of "we" and "us" makes it clear by the words you use that you consider yourself a part of the team. Not above or beyond them, but an essential member of the unit as a whole.

This reinforces that the team will share the benefits of

successful achievements, and also shares responsibility for failures.

How we speak influences how we think, and vice versa. Be intentional about the language you use and the effect those language choices can have on the longer-term development of your team and relationships.

Inclusive, versus exclusive. Together, instead of isolated.

Reinforce a shared sense of purpose that encourages the team to strengthen their bond and work better together. It moves them, and you closer to acting as a unit, instead of a loosely affiliated group of individuals.

———

Leaders Take Action

- *Are you comfortable sharing feedback (positive or negative) with your team? If not, why not?*
- *Brainstorm 5 ways you can change up how you share the results of success or failure with your team. Simple gratitude is often enough, but being creative here allows you to invent approaches that address any discomfort you identified above. In particular, around sharing negative feedback or the results of failure.*

PART III

STAY THE COURSE

INTRODUCTION

TRANSFORMING YOUR TEAM

In Part II of the book, we focused on you. Now, it's time to focus on your team.

While developing yourself to become an exemplary leader is a worthwhile investment in and of itself, genuinely exceptional results *at scale* are not achieved by merely setting a positive example.

To be an effective leader, you must take definitive and intentional actions to guide your team and empower them with the necessary support and structure they need to succeed.

I use the term team reasonably regularly throughout the book. I hope by now you've picked up on the fact that this may mean a team you have responsibility for or a group of independent people contracting on a project. It could also refer to your virtual assistant, your external vendors, or partners that work for your business.

Whatever the word team means for you, this section of the book is about helping you lead them to produce better, more valuable results. And, in doing so, to help them grow individually and as a unit.

We'll once again be exploring six key areas:

- **Motivation:** We'll explore how motivation differs for different people and the critical role it plays in team function.
- **Success:** While this book is not specifically about goal setting, our objective is to create and lead a successful team. To do that, we have to define success.
- **Failure:** As a leader, we need to change how we think about failure and how we use it to guide our team forward.
- **Personnel Changes:** Before we push our team to new heights, we first need to ensure that we have the right resources and level of commitment to get there.
- **Delegating Responsibility:** One of the critical skills for any team is a practical and effective ability to delegate work, and that starts with a solid understanding of responsibility.
- **Three Elements of Successful Delegation:** Delegating effectively can be one of the most challenging things for new managers to master, but the three elements we'll discuss in this chapter will set you on the path.

I have two goals for you as we work through this section together.

First, I want you to recognize that you don't have to do everything yourself.

Second, I want you to feel confident in knowing that your team is ready, willing, and able to take responsibility for their work — under your guidance and leadership.

12

UNDERSTANDING MOTIVATION

WHAT DRIVES YOUR TEAM?

I f you frequent the question and answer site Quora[1], there's a wealth of writers that debate the US Military, and the various branches of service.

The branches of the US Military love nothing more than to poke good-natured fun at each other. It's something of a sport in many cases.

You can also find more serious debates. The strategic importance of each service and its mission. Questions as to whether the Marines should be folded into the Army or Navy, or disbanded altogether.

The possibility of being disbanded has frustrated Marine Corps through much of its existence. Even after playing critical roles in the Pacific theater in World War II, it remained a political possibility.

After the raising of the flag on Mount Suribachi following the battle of Iwo Jima, Secretary of the Navy James Forrestal said, "The raising of that flag on Suribachi means a Marine Corps for the next 500 years."

Despite that prediction, a political battle to decide the

fate of the Corps still ensued, until the National Defense Act of 1947 cemented the Corps structure as it exists today.

This was not the first time the Marine Corps came face to face with its own possible extinction. To address this problem once and for all, the Marine Corps developed into what can only be called a marketing machine.

I don't make this reference in any negative light. It was, in my opinion, political and practical genius.

The campaign was simple enough in concept but certainly not in execution. A concerted effort was made to ensure that the value of the Marine mission was visible to the public eye, whenever and wherever possible.

Improving public perception, while mounting an effective political defense for their existence, had other benefits as well. It's those benefits to the organization that we'll focus on here.

The esprit de corps of Marines, the sense of self, can be admittedly a bit over-the-top, but it is hard to match in its intensity and effectiveness.

You see, Marines are deeply connected to what it means to be a Marine. The manifest level of motivation and engagement of Marines is hard to rival anywhere else. The Marine Corps encourages, even requires that level of dedication and pride of every Marine. By leveraging those elements to push Marines to higher achievement, and then putting that on public display, the Marine Corps solved its political problems. But, they also increased their capability and effectiveness.

That motivation, and dedication to the Corps, to the unit, is the driver that enables the accomplishment of things that often, by all rights, should be impossible. The Corps has always been smaller, less equipped, and underfunded.

They had to do more with less. And, the Marines have

consistently achieved that by ensuring that every Marine, from officer to enlisted, is highly motivated and dedicated to the completion of the mission.

I hope you'll excuse the impromptu, largely unqualified and completely biased history lesson. We Marines are a proud bunch.

If you want to effectively lead your team to accomplish things that initially seem impossible, you must understand what motivates them.

If you develop and foster motivation within your team, you can maintain the engagement necessary to accomplish the goals and objectives of your organization successfully, indefinitely.

Motivation and Engagement

We've discussed the benefit of motivation, the need for engagement, and how we can use one to drive the other.

But why exactly is engagement so critical?

Consider engagement as a measurement for each person on your team. A tank that we want to keep full. When engagement levels are high, that individual is connected to and excited about their work. When engagement is low, they pull back, their energy is down, their heart is just not in it, and they may be "phoning in" their efforts.

Think back on your past teams. Did you ever find your self less motivated, less engaged, pulling back from the job, or the work?

I certainly have.

Our goal then is to take a more intentional approach to the management of engagement. We need to actively determine and foster an environment with our team that is going to promote engagement. We have to understand why each individual on the team connects with their work. To discover how to best leverage and take advantage of their innate motivation to succeed.

This isn't a manipulative or controlling exercise on your part. If you get this right, it puts the individuals on your team in an ideal position to feel connected with and really enjoy their work and contribution.

It's a symbiotic, valuable exchange.

Finding Connection

How can we effectively identify what motivates a person and use that to guide them effectively?

The first step is to recognize that people connect with a task, a job, a team, or an organization for different reasons. We are not all motivated by the same things.

It's unrealistic to expect that the vision that energizes the executive team is going to motivate a junior team of software developers.

Let me give a hypothetical example.

Assume Acme Corp sells software widgets. The goals set by the board or executive leadership are likely to involve establishing the brand, capturing market share, and growing revenue.

The software team that develops those software widgets will connect differently with the organizational mission. Revenue and market share are many steps removed from the things they are asked to do day in and day out.

They are likely more interested in feature delivery, rate of bugs found in the widgets, customer satisfaction with the products they have produced.

I'm not implying that the big picture, the organizational mission, doesn't motivate people on the team just because they are not in an executive role. But, we need to consider the reality each individual faces as they fulfill their position on the team.

What work do they do on a day to day basis that they are proud of? Where do you often find an opportunity to give well-earned praise? Where is a need for correction or learning most prevalent?

We connect with things that directly impact us. The things that we do well, the things that we don't do well. The tasks that we are particularly good at and proud of as a contribution to our team. The further removed we are from something, the less impactful it becomes on our immediate reality.

The same is true in a factory, in a restaurant, or in a marketing agency.

The team's mission and unique characteristics of its members will determine how those people connect with the organization.

Recognizing this should not diminish any connection between the individuals and the organization. It should instead allow you to leverage day to day victories and acknowledge struggles unique to the team as you reinforce that connection to the broader organizational purpose.

It's our job as leaders to figure foster that connection between the team and the organization. To identify the connections that each person on the team forms with their work. To understand those connections, and to work them into the team culture.

To keep them highly engaged, but caring about the things that they care about. Building that engagement level, and maintaining it, will require that you find a balance that works for your team.

It may mean 20% of team engagement is driven by a connection to the organizational mission, and 80% comes from more tangible, direct accomplishments that align with the team's mission.

Your balance may be closer to 50/50 or 80/20.

Spend the time to learn that balance. Find that connection with the team, and then make an effort to align the team's motivation to the organizational mission. Do so in a way that keeps them, and you, excited and connected to what you are doing.

Avoid Competition

As you consider how you will build that connection, that motivation on your team, steer clear of one source of motivation that can have unintended consequences.

Competition can motivate individuals, but it can be a powerful negative force on your team.

As the team's leader, you are striving to create unity and cohesion, to encourage the team to work together. And, when challenged, to pull together and support each other.

Competition between individuals on the team will destroy this effort. When we're overly competitive and trying to win favor, position, or achievement as an individual positioned against our peers, we're not being incentivized to work as a team.

You want to drive engagement by encouraging connection with the things that matter most to each individual and the team as a unit. You also need to balance the needs of the individual against the success of the team as a group.

It's fine to encourage some competition between teams within the organization when kept positive this can certainly be healthy and often fun.

Just ensure the team is winning those competitions fairly, and as a team.

Leading people is often compared to herding cats: difficult bordering on impossible. But, if we understand what people want, what drives them to show up every day, we can provide and reinforce those things.

It enables us as leaders to connect the individuals on our team to something bigger. To focus on the organizational mission in a way that makes it easy for individuals to perform at their highest levels, and continue to push those boundaries upward.

———

Leaders Take Action

- *List at least 3 things that motivate or energize your team.*
- *List at least 3 things that would de-motivate or drain your team.*
- *Brainstorm at least 5 ideas that you can implement to help increase team engagement. These can be ways to increase or highlight the things that motivate your team. They could also be ways to avoid or minimize the things that de-motivate your team.*

13

PLAN FOR SUCCESS

In Part II, we discussed the need to evolve our mindset around success and failure and adjust our behaviors to share those outcomes, both positive and negative, with our teams.

In this chapter and the one that follows, we're going to revisit the topics of success and failure.

Effective leadership requires establishing a team culture that understands how success is defined, how success is achieved, and how success as a team is about more than getting things done.

It's about getting the *right* things done. And getting the right things done **at the right time.**

To do that, you need a plan. I don't mean a plan detailing how you will reach your goals or objectives. Not a plan for execution, but one for repeatable success.

A framework.

Planning for success means ensuring your team is taking intentional, considered action to achieve specific results. Establishing a framework to guide you through the process will help you do that.

If you, or your team, suffer from confusion, lack of understanding, or an unclear definition of what is expected, you are on a quick path to failure.

Successful planning can often be confusing for a new team or a new leader. We often look at our behaviors leading up to a negative outcome and think we were productive and working toward the goal.

But were we really? Were we doing the right things?

Adapting your success planning framework to encourage the team to evaluate their decisions and actions against goals or objectives can solve this.

Once we have the means to select the appropriate actions the team should take, we need to identify what measure defines success, and what timeline the team is expected to meet.

We'll cover a framework below that does just that. Before we do, let's make sure we don't fall into two common areas where the team can often appear successful, but really be failing.

Success as a Unit

The team must succeed or fail as a unit, success is achieved together or not at all.

The team that is carried to success by a minority of exceptional members may achieve the right outcomes, but is still failing in the broader sense. They are ignoring sustainability and growth in exchange for short term achievement.

How can you both succeed and fail?

When you lose sight of the forest for the trees.

When an individual works alone on objectives the group is responsible for, eventually, they will reach their limit or make a mistake. When that happens, they are not prepared to leverage the team to help mitigate failure.

They lack the resources and experience to adapt to an unexpected situation because they've set a precedent for working alone.

This also prevents the flow of knowledge and experience across the team that would promote faster growth of every team member, from the most junior to the most senior.

Remember, we're leading a team, not a loosely affiliated group of individuals.

Avoid Vanity Metrics

High-performing teams develop and use effective processes to achieve consistent results. This is expected. Figure out what works, then repeat that until it no longer works. Adapt and continue.

But, we must always understand that the perfect execution of the process alone is not a success.

If the team doesn't achieve the desired outcome or goals, that's a failure. Often, however, it can be unclear what we should be measuring.

We want to lead the team to succeed at the right things, and encourage a team culture that is comfortable questioning alignment to the vision and objectives. This enables an environment where everyone becomes accountable for the team's progress toward a shared understanding of our destination.

The trap to avoid is measuring the team's success using vanity metrics.

If you are an agile product team, your mastery of agile concepts and practices may be excellent, and you are consistently delivering new features. But if your product still doesn't provide a solution that meets the product vision, there is a problem.

Your team productivity metrics may be perfect, and your team always completes work on schedule. But if your objective results are lacking, there is a problem.

It's the difference between being busy and being productive.

We can't just assume if we are doing something and putting in the required amount of effort that the results become a foregone conclusion.

We have to do the right things.

How do we then effectively plan for success without falling into any of these problem areas?

We need a framework that helps us define success for our team and sets us on a path to achieve it.

I'm sure you are thinking, "Goal setting. You're going to talk to me about goal setting."

You don't need a framework for setting goals alone. You need something bigger. Something that helps you and your team agree on the vision. That establishes a strategy to achieve that vision, and then execute measure and improve your ongoing performance as you pursue that vision.

The framework I like to use for this is both simple and highly impactful. It consists of three stages: **Purpose, Planning**, and **Progress**.

Purpose

The first stage focuses on establishing a commonly understood purpose for the team. It also helps us answer some important questions.

What are we doing, and why are we doing it? How does

our team's purpose align with the broader vision and mission for the organization?

The purpose should be abstract, without being so obscure that it becomes ambiguous. Your goals should be objective and measurable. When you define the purpose, the level of detail should be closer to, "We'll know it when we get there."

Planning

In the planning stage, we do tackle goal setting. We aren't going to define exactly how you set and manage goals for your team as part of the framework. That is not the purpose of the planning stage.

Planning should be the creation of a strategic map that moves your team along the path from where they are towards the realization of the vision established in the purpose stage.

The vision is not entirely measurable, but more of a desirable future state that drives excitement and connection with your team. It's not directly actionable.

The planning stage uses that vision as a guide to identifying measurable, near-term goals that move the team in the right direction. Toward the desired end state, the ideal future state of achievement the team hopes to reach.

The outputs of your strategic planning should still represent the big picture. The critical points of your strategy should be milestones of achievement, not a punch list of tasks to be completed.

As you work with the team to identify your strategic plan, you'll outline key milestones or goals the team wants to reach.

For each goal set, the team should ask:

- Does this move us closer to our desired end state?
- Given what we know now, is this the most valuable and relevant milestone to pursue?

This is also the stage where you want to consider any risks, impediments, or dependencies — either internal to the team or external.

Use whatever goal setting and management system you or your team are comfortable with. If you haven't adopted one yet, try starting with SMART goals.

SMART goal setting criteria have been widely used for decades and can be interpreted and adjusted for different needs. Wikipedia offers a comprehensive overview of the variants and their origin. [1]

SMART goals for our framework should be:

- **Specific:** they target a particular outcome or area of improvement.
- **Measurable:** they can be objectively evaluated to determine success.
- **Achievable:** they are realistic, given the capabilities and constraints for the team.
- **Relevant:** they are related directly to the team's vision and long term objectives, and those of the organization.
- **Time-bound:** they are defined with a closed-end schedule that requires action to be successful.

Progress

The final stage in the framework takes us to execution. This is where the carefully planned work actually gets done.

We defined measurable goals as a required objective of our planning stage, and measurability is equally important as we begin executing.

How can we objectively measure the progress we are making?

The easy, albeit incorrect answer is that we can simply work toward our established goals and evaluate their success measures when complete.

The problem with this approach is that our goals are near-term but not immediate. Remember, they are milestones, not tasks. The issue with this is that we don't get the feedback we need soon enough to correct course or change behavior if something isn't working.

What is the team focused on doing this week? What are they focused on doing today to push towards the team objective? What impediments or problems do they see? How can they pull together as a group to address those?

What we need are measures that can help us predict if we are on going to meet our goals successfully or not.

There are two types of indicators we need to achieve this: **Lead Indicators** and **Lag Indicators**.

Lead indicators are measures that are known to predict future results. These measures also represent things that are in your control, or that you can directly affect.

Lag indicators conversely measure your end results. These are not things you can control directly, but they do quantify the results of the efforts measured by your lead indicators.

Let's use sales from an online store as an example.

As the store owner, I want to set goals related to monthly gross revenue. My sales pipeline consists of traffic to my store, converting traffic into successful sales, and my average cart value per purchase. This is an oversimplification, but it serves our purposes as an example.

If my conversion rate of traffic to buyers averages 25%, and my target gross revenue is $1,000 a day, I can quickly determine my lead and lag indicators.

In this scenario, I might choose traffic and average cart value as my lead indicators, and a trending daily revenue as my lag indicator.

With 100 visitors a day to my store, given my 25% conversion rate, 25 of those visitors will buy something. To hit my target daily revenue, with 25 buyers per day, I need to achieve an average cart value of $40.

100 x 0.25 x $40 = $1,000

My lead indicators here are traffic to the site and average cart value. These indicators are both things I can control that have a direct impact on my lag indicator: daily revenue.

I can control traffic to my side by using organic and paid strategies to drive people to my store.

I can control the average cart value by experimenting with my product offers to find combinations that make my customers happy and spend more money per order.

If my average order value is low, I can drive additional traffic to compensate.

If my traffic is stagnating or too expensive, I can plan on fewer visitors. By offering higher ticket items and adjusting my offers and products, my revenue goals are still achievable.

Taking action to improve my lead indicators will drive my lag indicator: daily revenue. Monitoring that daily revenue number will tell me if I'm on track to hit my monthly revenue goal, or not.

You can apply this same concept to any team or any type of work.

Review what your current goals require you to achieve and how that goal is measured. Establish lead indicators that will inform you whether you are on track or not on track toward the goals objectives when considering the time bounds applied to the goal.

Next, think about the tasks your team needs to complete to push the goal forward. What are indicators you can tie to that task completion that will measure controllable actions that drive results visible in your lag indicators?

Can the team clearly see the connection between the work selected for immediate action, the near term milestones or goals, and the team's purpose? Do your indicators reflect that link back to the purpose — is it clear that successful achievement of one leads to the other?

If something isn't well understood or doesn't seem to fit — challenge it and encourage the team to do the same.

The progress stage is an iterative experiment. One where we break our strategic plan down into actionable, consumable parts then figure out how to measure our execution. While executing, we pay attention to those measures, so we learn what works and what doesn't in a way that allows us to course-correct when necessary.

The end result is a framework of accountability that enables the team to discuss and improve how to approach their work. This evolves naturally in a way that guides them toward the successful completion of meaningful team objectives. It also provides you as the leader the ability to course-correct as priorities or even goals and purpose shift over time.

The framework helps to build the team's confidence by

establishing a clear link between planned daily actions, near term goals, and long term vision.

The outputs from the planning phase may produce rigid, detailed plans to achieve a distinct goal or milestone. The framework as a whole, however, provides a map to the successful realization of the team's responsibilities while still allowing for learning and adjustment.

Of course, the framework I've presented here is just one available option. If you choose to adopt something else, evaluate any framework you consider against the following requirements:

- Success metrics are well-defined and meaningful — no vanity metrics.
- Larger milestones are used to shape a plan that moves the team toward the vision. These milestones or goals should also serve to take somewhat ambiguous, possibly over-reaching, and often subjective targets and break them down into well-understood achievable items.
- Every milestone or goal has a clear alignment with the team's purpose.
- The plan includes an approach to ensure progress is being made, including lead and lag indicators where appropriate.

As the team leader, it is your responsibility to define and communicate the purpose, the strategic plan, and the approach to progressing toward realizing that plan. That doesn't (and shouldn't) prevent you from involving the team in its definition. The more you can successfully engage the group in establishing the plan, the more ownership they will feel in its successful achievement.

———

Leaders Take Action

- *On your own, define the purpose as you see it for your team.*
- *Now, with your team, explain the value that understanding the team purpose can bring and ask the team to define how they view the team purpose.*
- *As a group, compare your answer with theirs, and then collaborate on a final vision of team purpose that everyone agrees on.*
- *Review the Purpose, Planning and Progress framework with the team, or select a framework of your own. This can be a framework you already use, if applicable. Work with the team to ensure your approach to planning meets the required criteria we discussed earlier in the chapter.*

14

FAIL FORWARD

"Everybody has a plan until they get punched in the mouth"[12]

— MIKE TYSON

Neglect to plan for failure, and the most promising team may fall apart when facing its first significant challenge.

Even the best teams will fail.

Most well-orchestrated plans always have an element of risk. We will fail due to unexpected occurrences, unforeseen challenges, lack of experience, errors in judgment, and simple mistakes. This, of course, only scratches the surface of possible types and causes of failure.

Denying the possibility of failure, forging ahead confidently without acknowledging the risk, only ensures that when a failure occurs, your team will not respond well or recover gracefully.

Over analyzing and refining every plan to account for

every possibility, on the other hand, will drive progress to a halt. Analysis-paralysis is real.

How do we strike a balance that doesn't see our team completely unaware or unprepared for the unexpected without paralyzing our forward progress?

We need to change our mindset around failure, to recognize the probability of failure occurring, and forge ahead not blindly, but with a plan overcome any obstacles.

We start by understanding that failure is inevitable, and it is our job as leaders and professionals to mitigate the risk of failure and have a plan for recovery.

As a leader, you must remove the stigma of failure from the team. We, as people, are not perfect, and actions will occur that are both unforeseen and out of our control. By acknowledging, even expecting, that failure will happen, you position the team to react more favorably.

How do we do that?

We remove the fear of the unknown. As a team, we commit to learning from any mistakes and improving to prevent those same mistakes from recurring in the future.

We adopt a practice of failing forward.

The benefits of changing your team culture around failure in this way are not limited to improving the objective results the team produces. It also creates an environment that facilitates learning, growth, and the ability to take the calculated risks that drive innovation.

Let's explore a three-point framework you can use to add this approach to failure response into your team culture. As we encounter failures on our team, we'll consider the three points of the ERR framework: **Evaluate, Recover, Refine.**

Evaluate

Evaluating any failure to understand the intent behind the actions taken by your team.

Right or wrong, you need to understand why one particular action was chosen over another. Does the intent behind the choice align with the team's vision and goals? If the purpose behind the work is well aligned, there's a real learning opportunity to determine why the actions didn't deliver the expected results.

If the intent is not aligned, a discussion needs to take place to understand why the team strayed from the vision and goals, intentionally.

Your observations as you evaluate the failure, the actions that were taken, and the reasons behind those actions will inform your path as you and the team move forward.

If the team deviated from the agreed purpose intentionally, it's essential to discuss and understand why. Does the agreed vision need to change? Was the purpose unclear or otherwise misunderstood?

Understanding and discussing the intent behind choices you and the team have made will set the stage to have a productive discussion about what can be learned from the experience.

Recover

How day you react to failure? How long does that reaction go on? Are you in control, or do your emotions take over? At what point do you start recovering and moving forward?

These are hard questions to ask yourself, but necessary none the less. It's essential for you to understand your own reaction and recovery behaviors, so you can then evaluate and coach these same behaviors within your team.

That reaction we have to failure is a natural response. We can't suppress it, any more than we can stop ourselves from breathing.

What we can control is how long we let it go on. Reacting is natural, but when we embrace that reaction and ride the downward spiral, that is a choice.

And, it's a choice we don't have to keep repeating.

The recover attribute of the framework reminds us to focus on the team on a positive forward movement, and not to get hung up on what went wrong and why beyond the value that evaluating that failure can bring.

Guide your team to move past the failure and on to the next success.

Refine

Actual failure occurs not when we miss an achievement or fall short of a goal. It happens when we fail to learn from those events.

Or, when we quit — but you aren't a quitter.

The refinement step allows you and your team to take the results of evaluating and discussing failure as an opportunity to improve and prevent a future occurrence.

In this step, we facilitate a discussion among the team with the distinct goal of identifying specific changes to process, practices, or behaviors.

Don't overthink this. We don't have to solve everything in one pass. Solve the most critical or well-understood item first.

James Altucher suggests trying to improve 1% every day.

If we compound that improvement over your team will have grown 3,800% after a year.[3]

You don't have to boil the ocean. Seek consistent improvement, not perfection.

As you reflect and review after any failure, there are, however, a few root causes that you need to pay special attention to:

- **Attitude:** A single lousy attitude on your team can sink the whole ship. If you find members of the team that are hard to work with, or that are willfully negligent in their behaviors, you need to consider whether to remove them.
- **Ego:** Similarly, there is no room for ego on your team. An outsized ego will kill any ability you have to make the team function as a unit. There's no room for improvement as a team when individuals are too focused on their own accomplishments and need for individual recognition.

If you identify a pattern of failures that indicates one or more members of your team is a poor fit, you need to take responsibility to remove that person. We'll revisit how to prepare yourself to tackle that in the next chapter.

Embrace the certainty of failure. Adopt it as a part of your team culture. Plan for the unexpected, and you will not be caught completely unprepared when it occurs. Most importantly, demand not perfection from your team but continuous improvement.

If you can master the application of this framework to resolve and respond to failure, over time, your team will build confidence and trust in the process that enables them to fail forward successfully.

———

Leaders Take Action

- *Consider how you react to failure now. This can mean missed deliverables, failed projects, or whatever failure means as your team is measured. List any reactions you know you exhibit that are negative or counter-productive.*
- *For each item above, brainstorm 5 ways you can turn this around and respond in a productive, positive way that pushes the team forward.*

15

THE POSITIVE EFFECT OF PERSONNEL CHANGES

As a manager, one set of critical skills you will often be required to perform is the evaluation and recommendation or decision to hire or fire personnel.

Depending on the size of your organization and level of responsibility, the final decision may not be yours. Still, you should absolutely be screening, interviewing, and making recommendations for every role that is filled or vacated on your team.

If you lead a team currently but aren't participating in the hiring or termination process, you should consider how you can start playing a more active role based on what you learn here.

Then, work with your organization to make that happen.

Of course, there are pure management roles where the team you have to work with is assigned to you. If you are in one of those roles now, changing the process may not be possible.

Ideally, however, the organization will recognize the value of accepting your input and advice on the make-up of your team. I hope that by now, *you* realize the impact you will have in your role by being a leader, and not only a manager.

If you find yourself in a situation where you lack control over the staffing of your team, the positive personnel change you may want to consider is moving into another organization that places a higher value on your input and ability to make critical decisions.

Ultimately, when you accept responsibility for leading a team, you must work to ensure you have the tools and resources you need to be successful. The most effective place to start is to evaluate the strengths and weaknesses of your team. Based on the results of that evaluation, you must be willing *and able* to leverage personnel changes as a positive and powerful tool to build the team and environment that you need to produce successful results.

It's Not Easy

Hiring and firing people is never easy, nor should it be. It's challenging to evaluate and find the right people for a given role. It's even more difficult when you have to remove someone that is not working out.

I have hired people that met and often exceeded all the expectations established during the interview process. I've also mistakenly hired people that seemed like they were a good fit, only to discover later that they were not. They just didn't work out. Despite your best efforts during the screening process, sometimes you will be wrong.

I've interviewed people for a role where it felt nearly impossible to make a decision because the candidates were all fantastic. Finding and working with amazing people is undoubtedly one of the high points of personnel management.

Of course, the low point is when you have to let someone go.

Maybe you missed something in the screening process. Perhaps the person started out promising and productive, and something changed over time, and their work started to suffer. We all have our ups and downs in life, and sometimes, try as we might to avoid it, these things bleed into our professional space.

When this occurs, ideally, we have the latitude to be compassionate, and the courage to be realistic and fair to our team as a whole. We need to demonstrate empathy, but there are limits we have to respect and enforce.

People will surprise you with their reactions to being let go. They've certainly surprised me.

I've fired people whose reactions were mostly indifferent, or who at least wished to appear so in the moment.

I've also had to terminate people that were gracious and understanding, despite the tears in their eyes that showed the emotional impact they were trying unsuccessfully to hide but still would not voice.

Your responsibility as a leader is to decide what you believe to be right for everyone involved. How you execute that responsibility will vary based on the circumstances and individuals involved.

People will surprise you, but there is a guiding principle that can help you navigate this challenging task successfully: Respect.

Respect the magnitude, the impact that this type of change can have on someone's life. This applies equally when you are hiring someone into your team, or when you are removing them from it.

How often have you heard someone speak of their work as if it isn't overly important to them?

"It's just a job, it's not who I am."

I don't disagree with this sentiment, you are not your job. But, separating ourselves from our work is not so simple. We spend so much of our adult lives at our jobs that while we may not want to let our work define us, it certainly has an effect on who we are and who we become.

How can it not? You probably spend the majority of the hours of every week working.

Whether we like it or not, what we do, and how we spend our time becomes a part of who we are. And, when we as managers step into that room to hire or fire someone, we are making a potentially monumental change to their life.

Respect that responsibility.

Hiring can be hard to get right. Firing people is just plain hard. Neither task should be easy, nor can they be taken lightly.

Don't Procrastinate or Over Compromise

As awkward or uncomfortable as making hiring or termination decisions may feel, it's critical that you neither delay or rush through the process.

It's natural to want to put unpleasant or stressful things to be put behind us. Like ripping off a band-aid, we just want it to be over as quickly and painlessly as possible.

The benefits of successfully locating, screening, and onboarding key hires for your team should be readily apparent. The impact when you are unable to fill open hiring requests is equally easy to understand. When there is more work to be done than resources available, both the team's progress toward their objectives and their morale will suffer.

It's this recognition of the impact a lack of resources

creates that can drive us to make poor decisions in hiring. If you find yourself rushing through hiring decisions or selecting compromise candidates simply to get a warm body into an open role, you are neglecting to think about the longer-term effects this can have on your team.

The culture of your team and that of the broader organization is affected by every hire you make. When you make concessions for a compromise candidate, you are introducing a change to the culture, and that change may not be desirable.

In the worst cases, it can be toxic to your team.

Clashes between individuals on the team will impact team morale. Whether from personality clashes or a perceived skills gap with the new hire, the team will be affected as they try to adapt to the change.

Lowered team morale leads to lower motivation, and left unchecked can lead to lower engagement.

I'm not suggesting that you should avoid hiring imperfect people. We are all imperfect people. Trust your judgment, and consider why you are considering the candidate for the role. Consider how they would both impact and integrate with the team.

Don't ruin a stellar team that you've worked hard to form by trying to solve short term resourcing needs by making poor hiring decisions and ignoring that individual's lack of culture fit or long term performance potential.

Resourcing concerns can also affect our decisions when it comes to removing a problematic team member. Often we may be tempted, or even decide, to keep on a team member that is underperforming, or worse yet, causing conflict on the team because we feel we can't afford to lose them as a resource. If the group is already understaffed, whether due to lack of hiring or recent departures, removing another person can feel like a step in the wrong direction.

I would remind you again that your decisions or any delay in making those decisions can have a long term impact on the team. The team culture, individual morale, and eventually, motivation and engagement will suffer.

While it may seem like a better choice to leave an under-performing person on the team when compared to having no one in the role at all, often, this is not the case. When you've formed a team culture that embraces success and failure as a unit and not as individuals, the weak links tend to stand out.

Your responsibility is to empower the team to be successful.

Again, I'm not suggesting you set standards that require perfection. But, once you've identified someone unable or unwilling to grow into their role and be a valuable member of the team, it's your responsibility to remove them.

Don't ruin a stellar team that you've worked hard to form by trying to solve short term resourcing needs by delaying difficult decisions and ignoring that individual's lack of culture fit or long term growth potential.

How Can Being Fired Be Positive?

The positive benefits to the team of removing underper-forming or otherwise problematic people should be reason-ably clear and easy to understand.

As uncomfortable as the task may be, it's our responsi-bility as leaders.

To make this difficult task somewhat more manageable, consider the problem not only from the team perspective but also from the perspective of that individual employee.

Each of us as individuals has our own goals, and when we're in a role or position where we can't reach those goals, it's as difficult for us as it is for our team. As leaders, it's our responsibility to correct these problems. We must do this, both for the benefit of the group and the individual.

Will this always be an achievable outcome? No, of course not.

Some people will cross lines that force your hand and don't allow for any kind of positive transition. With problems of severe attitude, insubordination, or outright refusal to perform the duties of the job, you have to put the team's needs first.

Rip off that band-aid quickly, and move on.

For the more rational, professional individuals that we still need to transition out of our teams, however, we have an opportunity to use termination as a tool for growth.

Satisfaction with our jobs, which impacts satisfaction in our life, stems from being in a role where we can be successful. As you adopt the principles, we've been exploring, you will develop an ability to recognize personnel problems early. You'll know when someone has either a skills gap or is exhibiting a poor personality fit. And, you'll realize when those limitations are going to impact their career negatively.

Work with the individuals on your team to ensure that when you identify such a gap, they can see it as well. Set clear expectations for what is expected of that person in that role.

A quick litmus test to determine if both you, and the individual in question have established a shared understanding of expectations for their role is to answer these three questions:

- Do you understand your responsibilities on the team?
- Do you know where you can get help when you need it?
- Do you understand how success is measured for your role?

When you and the individual agree on these points but still see a gap in performance, the nature of the conversation changes. Instead of discussing failures in what often will feel like a personal attack, we can now address the misalignment of skills or behaviors.

This enables us to ensure that we don't abandon our responsibility as a leader to coach, mentor, and advise the people on our team the minute we decide they are not an ideal fit. It gives us the tools we need to either help them close those gaps between expectation and reality or manage their transition off of the team. Sometimes that may mean a move to another team in the organization. Others may require separation from the organization altogether. In either case, we continue to help and support them, just as we would for any other member of your team.

In this way, removing someone from a role does not always have to be a punitive action. Often the right approach is to identify a problem before it spirals out of control and work with that person to help them either grow into the role or find a position that, in the long term, will help them be more successful and happier in their work.

This is the most ideal outcome you can work towards, but it does require consistent and continuous work. As you lead your team, the focus you place on establishing a clear vision, guiding the team culture, and changing attitudes around success and failure work to create the environment you need to turn this often unpleasant responsibility into a positive tool.

Forming and maintaining a team comprised of the right people in the right roles is critical to our success as leaders. It's equally important that we realize the benefits of termination and the risks of hiring too quickly.

Remember that the most essential component of personnel management is not management, but people.

Focus on identifying a path where people can be successful, and feel fulfilled in their professional life, and guide your personnel decisions accordingly. Do this successfully, and the objective results you need your team to deliver will *almost* take care of themselves.

Leaders Take Action

- *Consider your current behaviors or thoughts concerning personnel management. Do you consider it a positive and necessary tool to manage your team? Why, or why not?*
- *Brainstorm 5 ideas you can implement to change or improve your approach to personnel management based on what you've learned here. Be creative and consider how you may need to adjust your techniques to develop a team culture where you can remove people not only for the benefit of the team but for the individual as well.*

16

DELEGATING RESPONSIBILITY

"The difficulty of a task has no bearing on your responsibility to complete it."

— MATTHEW OVERLUND

Yes, I just quoted myself. I hope you don't mind.

This will be the first of two chapters that collectively address the delegation of work to your team. It's an important topic and one that, if neglected, can severely impact your ability to lead your team successfully.

You see, while I would be happy to hear you've shared the quote above with your team, I've included it here for *you*.

As a leader, you have a responsibility to your team to manage the delegation of work and to ensure the team has the resources, capabilities, and time to complete that work successfully.

The more complex the objectives of your team, the harder this task often becomes. But, even relatively simple assignments can present a management challenge as you attempt to balance the work and dependencies for that work across the team.

The difficulty of the task has no bearing on your responsibility to complete it. The same principle applies to your team and forms the basis for how we will approach delegation.

We could simply break down our team's objectives into tasks and divide the assignment of those tasks across our available resources. Sometimes this is the appropriate approach. Often, however, if we are expected to build a high-performing, high-value team, we need a different tactic.

We need to assign responsibilities, not tasks alone.

Wait a minute, didn't I just get done telling you that your responsibilities belong to you, regardless of how difficult they might be?

Absolutely.

Your responsibility is to delegate *areas of responsibility* to your team effectively. If your organization is smaller, you may retain ownership of some of the work directly. If your team is more extensive, you may manage other leaders who, in turn, break down their areas of responsibility for delegation to *their* organizations.

Leading by delegating responsibility provides us the structure to scale up our organizational structure as it becomes necessary. Attempting to scale up a team that operates based on delegation of tasks is much harder, often impossible.

Why?

Assigning responsibility means ensuring someone understands and agrees to produce the desired outcome. That person accepts responsibility for something, regardless of the difficulty of the tasks required for completion.

When we assign responsibility, we don't dictate how the work should be achieved, only what must be completed, and when we expect it. We agree on the objective outcome, not on the steps that will be taken to reach it. This innate flexibility, or autonomy, allows us to step back from the required work, leaving it to the person we've trusted with its completion. This frees us up to manage other areas of the team, or take on other necessary work. We will cover this topic in more detail in the next chapter.

Assigning tasks, on the other hand, means telling someone to do something specific, and then managing their execution of that task through to completion. We don't relinquish any responsibility, which in turn leaves no room for the person doing the work to exercise their own judgment as to how the work should be completed.

When you assign responsibility for both how an objective should be reached as well as the execution, the responsible person can apply their own experience and capabilities to achieve the goal. They are more likely to hold themselves accountable for an approach to meeting the given challenge when they had a hand in producing that approach.

For your team, days filled with task execution do not promote a feeling of ownership. That lack of ownership will impact motivation. While the ability to follow instructions is necessary and commendable, it won't provide an environment that encourages individual growth or pride in accomplishment.

As a manager, relying on delegation based on task assignment alone puts you at risk of straying into the realm of micro-management. When you assign tasks but don't share the associated responsibility, it becomes challenging to create separation between yourself and the work being done. This can quickly become a slippery slope to micromanagement. One where you find yourself unable to avoid checking on progress, offering unsolicited advice, or any of several other practices that will frustrate your team.

In a previous chapter, we discussed a 3-step framework to help your team define and execute towards goals that are well-aligned to the team's mission. Establish and explain the purpose, plan goals or milestones around objective results that move towards the achievement of that purpose, and track progress by monitoring the metrics that matter.

If you struggle to differentiate the delegation of tasks and responsibility, consider the problem as an extension of the Purpose, Planning, and Progress framework.

Ask yourself: Are you delegating work that is defined in the planning step, or the progress step?

If you are only assigning work that needs to be executed toward an objective that you have defined and retain responsibility for, you are assigning tasks.

If you assign responsibility for meeting a measurable, but complex objective, and you share responsibility for both defining and executing the solution, then you are assigning responsibility.

We've been working towards this point in your development as a leader, progressively chapter by chapter. This is the point at which you put it into practice.

Trust, motivation, and engagement set the stage for the team to accept responsibility for critical objectives. By developing a team culture that pursues actions specifically to achieve goals that are well aligned with the team's mission or vision, the unit removes distractions and increases their efficiency. Planning for the possibility of failure and establishing an approach to mitigating, learning from, and moving forward when it occurs means that your team won't fall apart when challenged by the unexpected. Taking responsibility for actively managing personnel means you've removed distractions and ensured that the team has the resources they need to be successful.

Despite all of this, you may still be struggling with the need to let go of responsibility. Let's address that now.

You may be worried that the team won't be able to do the job as well as you could yourself, or at the very least, that they won't reach that level of performance without your direct guidance.

If you are struggling with this, remind yourself to trust your team and trust that you've made the right decisions in staffing that team. You may be correct in your evaluation that the team won't perform the work as you could or would. Realize, however, that by taking a leadership role, you can develop the right group of people such that they exceed your own capabilities, often many times over.

You may struggle with a feeling that your value declines when you aren't directly doing the work. You may *enjoy* doing the work and find it hard to let go for that reason.

Consider, once again, the effect of scale. The value you bring to the organization or business with your skills and expertise will be multiplied many times over as you guide, mentor, and coach your team to new accomplishments. Your personal delivery of value has not declined, it has only shifted to another outlet.

You may feel uncomfortable assigning work to your team because you believe that they can't successfully complete the job.

To address this, return to your framework for planning. Ensure you are including the team when establishing the purpose and defining your milestones. Leverage the trust you've built with the team to facilitate open communication.

Drive conversation that evaluates the activities required to successfully complete the work against the team's capacity and the necessary time of completion for each objective. The effort you've made to establish a positive culture that is focused on the entire team's success will support you as you work through these doubts.

Responsibility is often equated to power, and it can be challenging to relinquish if we view it as a loss of status. Still, we must consider that if we share none of the responsibility, we are denying that sense of achievement from our team.

In short, if you want your team to produce amazing results, you first have to give them opportunities with potential.

Assigning responsibility means defining what must be done and when it should be complete. Leaving the specifics to be decided and worked by the team promotes the development of problem-solving skills, creative thinking, and a feeling of ownership of the results — positive or negative.

This can be a frightening prospect as a leader. However, it is our job to find a way to effectively delegate ownership to our team while still driving successful results.

That is our responsibility, and we can complete it, no matter how difficult it may seem at first.

———

Leaders Take Action

- *Do your team's objective responsibilities and structure make it easier to delegate tasks or responsibilities?*
- *Do you feel that your team connects well and feels a*

sense of ownership with their work? If not, what is the primary cause?

- *Brainstorm 5 ideas you want to try that will help build a sense of ownership on the team, as they take on more responsibility and less specific task work.*

17

THREE ELEMENTS OF SUCCESSFUL DELEGATION

As a leader, you are responsible for preparing your team to execute delegated responsibilities successfully and effectively. To do this, you must empower them with the tools they need to be successful. It starts with sharing responsibility. However, once we've done this, we also must provide the team with the tools they need to fulfill that responsibility.

There are three critical elements to successful delegation. Together they represent a simple framework that allows us to delegate responsibility and let go of direct control, yet still, achieve results expected of our team and us. Doing so requires us to strike a careful balance where we support our team without crossing a threshold into micromanaging.

This is a challenge that is, unfortunately, all too often neglected or ignored. It may be more comfortable, certainly in the short term, to simply step in and "get the job done" rather than stand by and watch as our team tries to work through challenges they encounter.

Obviously, this is a short term mindset and one that does little to facilitate growth. That is not to say that sometimes it's not necessary, depending on the circumstances. Still, we should also ensure that when we make the decision to step in and take direct action to complete work that our team should ultimately be responsible for, we recognize that we are limiting their future capability.

It is a trade-off — and one we need to be both aware of and intentional about accepting if we are to use it wisely.

Autonomy

The first element of our framework is autonomy. This is the freedom of action that we must grant to our team for them to evaluate, plan, and execute the work necessary for them to fulfill their responsibilities.

As a strong leader with your own areas of expertise, it can be challenging to step back and let your team figure things out for themselves. It is, however, this process of discovery and problem solving that encourages growth. There is a delicate balance we must strike between leaving the individuals on our team the space they need to operate and sharing our knowledge and experience to provide them the guidance they may require. Still, as difficult as this balance may be to achieve, it is essential that we avoid crossing a line where we slip back into doing ourselves those things that we should instead be guiding to completion with our team.

Sometimes this can mean you need to leave space in the room intentionally. In our haste to be helpful, and often driven by the natural empathy we feel as we see others struggle with something that we think we can assist with, we can overlook the unintended consequences of our help or even our presence.

Leave space in the room. Whether you and your team-work in the same physical office, or you connect remotely from different geographic locations, consider the effect of your presence when the team is working through a task, or when you are participating in a group meeting.

You need to be aware of the effect your inherent authority and experience can have on the team. Often more junior people can feel intimidated or uneasy, leading them to avoid offering suggestions or speaking up in a group setting.

Similarly, as you develop the leadership capabilities of the individuals on your team, you need to leave them comfortable space to exercise and grow those capabilities. If we are overly directive, or sometimes even just too helpful, it can leave the team in a position where they feel everything has been said or already been handled in such a way that there is no need for them to speak up, get involved, or offer suggestions.

Consider the mix of personalities on your team and adjust accordingly to ensure the people you've trusted with delegated responsibility have the freedom to explore solutions to challenges they are presented with as they work to meet those responsibilities. Some people will need you to draw them out and encourage them to share their opinions or thoughts. Others will act autonomously and speak freely without prompting but may withdraw if you've already stepped in and solved or spoken to an issue.

How you manage this will rely heavily on the relation-ships and understanding of various individuals on your team. You will need to make an effort to balance between remaining out of the way, and ensuring you are providing the necessary support and assistance when it is required and requested.

The easiest way to achieve this is to regularly seek ways to reinforce and continue to build trust with your team so that the individuals in question have the confidence to act autonomously. This confidence grows from an understanding that you are available as a resource when needed, will support their efforts made as they execute their responsibilities, and ultimately that you trust them to do the job.

Authority

Along with granting a balanced level of autonomy to your team comes the necessity to pair that autonomy with an appropriate level of authority.

Authority and autonomy are closely related. You have to trust your team with the necessary authority they will require to successfully complete their responsibilities, without inserting yourself as a central point of authority that must make every decision. Empowering your team to execute their duties successfully means providing the tools and environment they need to be successful. If you, as the leader, are guarding the necessary authority to make every decision, then you have made your team responsible in name only.

Our goal as leaders should be to evolve our team to an ideal state where we can both share responsibility and share authority, with appropriate boundaries in place.

Don't position yourself as a central point of authority that must either make or approve every decision.

Doing so undermines autonomy and devalues the assignment of responsibility. Consider the effect on an individual that is attempting to complete work they are responsible for when any decision of any consequence must be reviewed and approved by someone else. It is not a scenario that builds or communicates trust.

It also forces you to ask yourself how effective your efforts at hiring, mentoring, and coaching have been. If you feel the risk of delegating authority to your team is too high, you may be hiring at inappropriate levels of skill or experience. If you've made the intentional decision to hire entry-level employees, but you never reach a point where you feel confident in granting them a controlled level of authority, you may be failing to develop the individuals on your team to their full potential.

Your responsibility as a leader includes both selecting and developing the right resources into the roles you need to build a capable team. If you've assembled a team that you can't share authority with, you may have missed the mark entirely, or at the very least, created a flat authority structure that will limit you to being a pure manager that can only effectively delegate tasks.

Strike a balance between providing support or validation of the decision-making process, and retaining responsibility for those decisions that fall outside the bounds of authority your team may be comfortable taking on. Obviously, you should also keep any authority for which you, as the team leader, are expected to remain both accountable and responsible. Promote growth within the team, but don't wholly abandon good judgment to be over-inclusive.

We want to push the boundaries of the team to encourage growth, not leave them feeling abandoned by forcing them to assume authority that is too far outside their comfort or experience level.

The critical measure of success can be reduced to two questions:

- Are you delegating responsibility to the team with no authority?
- Have you delegated *all* of your own authority to the team?

If you answer yes to either question, you likely need to reevaluate your approach.

Accountability

That which is measured improves, and accountability provides the structure to measure the performance of an individual against assigned responsibilities.

As a leader, this is your most reliable tool to help your team understand what a successful outcome is, and reiterate the importance of the responsibility they've been assigned.

We achieve this by establishing objective goals, with clear expectations and well-defined timelines.

Accountability and responsibility go hand in hand. Ideally, we assign responsibility to individuals on our teams in areas where they are interested and engaged. As we encourage our team to assume responsibility for things they want to work on and take ownership of, our team culture should reinforce that each individual is accountable to the group as a whole for the work they take on.

In a team sports setting, you would more commonly talk about teamwork. I don't view the two concepts as significantly different.

As we delegate work across our team, we scale the team's capability up. We usually achieve this by dividing work across multiple resources. The challenge is that sharing work often does nothing to reduce the original dependencies of the resulting smaller work items. The objective deliverable the team must produce remains the same as if a single person were doing the work. A failure in one of the delegated work items often means failing the entire objective.

In soccer, the goalie is responsible or guarding the team's goal and trying to prevent the opposing team from scoring. If the goalie decides to wander off in the middle of a game, the team's chance of winning just took a significant hit.

Our wayward goalie had responsibility for defending the goal but didn't recognize or care to acknowledge their accountability to the team or the effect their performance would have on the shared objective for the group as a whole.

As the team's leader, you need to encourage them to adopt this understanding of accountability in a way that promotes communication and trust between each individual and you as the team's leader.

We need to reinforce that being part of a team requires teamwork for the team to be successful and that as we accept responsibility for something, we are now accountable to something larger than ourselves.

In this way, accountability becomes both a tool for management and a guiding principle for the individual.

Accountability occasionally gets something of a negative reputation. It is often associated with a punitive attitude around the completion of work.

In my opinion, this is not the ideal use of this valuable tool. After all, how often do you find yourself motivated to complete work if the driving factor for doing so is simply to avoid punishment?

Accountability should be about respect and consideration for the people on your team. As we learn to rely on each other, we naturally expect personal accountability from each other.

It is the basis on which we build the ability to successfully function as a unit, rather than a loosely affiliated group of individuals that may wander off the soccer field at an unfortunate time.

Learning to lead by growing your team to produce successful outcomes where you aren't making every decision, or touching every task can seem daunting at first. But, mastering the key elements necessary to empower the individuals on your team to effectively execute delegated responsibility is the hallmark of a true leader.

***

Leaders Take Action

- *Do you struggle with letting go, or stepping back to leave room for the individuals on the team to step up or be more self-directive? If so, why?*
- *Brainstorm 5 ideas you can try that will help you grant a higher level of autonomy to your team.*
- *As a result of taking a step back to allow your team to work, what are your biggest fears?*
- *Brainstorm 5 ideas you implement that would allow you to leverage positive non-punitive forms of accountability to mitigate your fears.*
- *Are teamwork and personal accountability synonymous on your team? If not, list the reasons why you feel there is a breakdown. Communication*

failures, personality conflicts, lack of personal accountability, etc.

- *For each break down listed above, brainstorm 5 ways you want to try that may improve the situation. If the areas of break down are not overly severe, make this a group activity.*

PART IV

ANCHORS AWEIGH

INTRODUCTION

TRANSFORMING THE FUTURE

In the previous two sections of the book, we've covered a lot of ground.

As you have no doubt noticed, this book is not overly prescriptive. I can't tell you the closely guarded secrets that, once mastered, will make you an ideal leader.

They don't exist.

I can only share my experiences and learnings on the topic in a way that sets you on the path. In some ways learning to lead is about being able to see that path. Not everyone can.

Once you see the path, and you commit to setting yourself on it, you've begun a long journey. One that will, if done right, consume the rest of your life.

To lead, you must be willing to change, to take risks, to be the first to experience something, and then share that experience with others.

But, I don't want to leave you unprepared for the journey ahead, and in this section, we're going to explore 6 topics that will help you answer the question: "What's next?":

- **Determine Your Path:** If your leadership journey were a climb up Mount Everest, this chapter is where you establish your base camp.
- **Professional Development:** Leadership bestows a responsibility to continue learning and developing yourself.
- **Board of Advisors:** What is a "board of advisors," and why do you need one?
- **Mentoring & Coaching:** What's the difference, and when is the right time to engage?
- **Prepare Your Replacement:** In this chapter, I will challenge you to do something that will feel unconventional at first, and then I'll show you why it works and is the best thing for you.
- **Continuous Improvement:** the reward for work well done is generally a higher volume of more complex work being assigned to you and your team. In this chapter, we will explore the concept of continuous improvement, and how working it into your team culture enables you to meet any challenge without overwhelm.

This is an exciting phase, as you consider your development as a leader.

This is where you take the knowledge, self-inspection, and transformational changes you've introduced into your team and your approach to leadership, and you start to think about new possibilities.

You will discover new paths that you weren't previously prepared to lead your team down that now feel achievable.

18

DETERMINE YOUR PATH

"Management is efficiency in climbing the ladder of success; leadership determines whether the ladder is leaning against the right wall."[1]

— STEPHEN COVEY

Now that you have a solid understanding of the strategic problems we are trying to solve as we grow into our role as leaders, let's make sure your ladder of growth is set against the right wall.

Finding Your Values

When I work with a new coaching client, the exercise we'll explore in this chapter is usually one of the first that I introduce. So, why are we only getting to it now, toward the end of the book?

"When the student is ready, the teacher will appear"[2]

— Lau Tzu

I needed to ensure that we have a good understanding between us of the problems we are trying to solve. By this point, you have a good familiarity with the areas that you need to focus on as you learn to *lead* rather than *do*. Now that you know what you are trying to solve, I want you to take some time to consider your values.

Doing so at this point in your journey enables you not just to think about what you value, but to consider your values in light of what is, hopefully, a new perspective on your role as a leader.

By evaluating your values as a professional and as a leader, you unlock the ability to set clear goals and establish a plan to meet them. Recognizing your values, what motivates and drives you to improve will empower you to achieve more fulfilling and valuable targets.

What makes your values so crucial in the context of your professional development and growth?

Recall in the last section where we explored the effect of motivation on our team and the need to monitor and promote motivation if we want to maintain engagement?

The same need exists for you. Hopefully, have a good relationship with your own manager. And that they are looking after your motivation and engagement. As a leader, however, this is an area where we have to commit to a certain level of self-care.

Nothing will destroy your ability to effectively lead than a lack of engagement with your role or with your team. It comes down to one simple point: you have to care about the people around you, and what you are collectively trying to achieve.

Regardless of how well you feel you can fake it — and sometimes we all have to fake it, everyone has an off day — you can't successfully do so over an extended time and expect your team not to realize that you aren't really present or engaged.

So, back to our question: why are our values so closely tied to our professional development?

Your values and ability to align those values with your role becomes the tool by which you manage your engagement. When your values are not aligned with your activities, your stress levels naturally rise, and over time stress and misalignment of values will drive your level of motivation and engagement down.

Put simply, whether we admit it to ourselves or not, we aren't psychologically wired to act against our nature for an extended period. At least not without any adverse effects.

I'm not suggesting that people can't change, or that people's values may not change over time — but when that happens, you can be sure that you will inevitably change your patterns of behavior, up to and including significant life-altering decisions.

How many stories, movies, or even real-life experiences have you encountered where you were taught that it can be challenging to remain true to your values, to who you are, when faced with external pressures?

We learn about peer pressure as kids. I grew up in the '80s, so for me, peer pressure was embodied by the Nancy Reagan era ads to Say No to Drugs. "This is your brain on drugs." Apparently, our brains in the '80s were a fried egg. If you weren't old enough to enjoy these ads live on TV, you could relive them through the magic of the internet. [3]

As challenging as it can be to avoid external pressure, we often forget to apply the same rigor to ourselves. It's easy to fall into patterns of behavior that are driven by what we feel we need to do or should be doing, and we fail to consider our values as we commit ourselves to a particular job, goal or course of action.

Inevitably, we find ourselves in the same position as we would if we had allowed an external influence to drive a course of action that is counter to our values: we disengage, become frustrated or stressed, and generally struggle to find happiness.

Setting aside self-destructive or self-sabotaging behavior, sometimes we simply do this because we don't realize the problem. I've discussed the need to be intentional as a leader previously, and I'm going to repeat that here. You need to be intentionally introspective about defining your values. The exercise of forcing yourself to think about them, refine, and record them will bring them front of mind and encourage you to be more intentional about shaping your future choices to be in alignment with those values.

The point here is simply (or not so simply) to understand ourselves better so we can make more informed decisions about the actions we take. This allows us to move beyond avoiding particular activities because we just don't like them, and instead start to understand why we don't enjoy that activity.

From that understanding, we can then make more rational decisions, such as when to delegate, and to whom, based on a solid understanding of why we are not the right person for a particular task.

As we grow our understanding of our own behaviors and actions stemming from our values, we also learn to recognize the same in others.

Now that you understand why connecting to your core

values is essential, I want to dispel some common confusion around what we actually mean by values.

Let's start with an explanation of three commonly related concepts that fiction writers explore as they work to develop and understand a new character.

Fictional characters are, by definition, not real people. Consider the books, movies, or plays that have impacted you the most, that effect you deeply every time you experience them. The characters feel as real as you or I. This is because the author has done the work to create a realistic, believable, *human* character complete with their own beliefs, value system, strengths, and yes, flaws.

As a character for a new work evolves, the author often tries to understand their goals, ambitions, and values.

Goals are well-understood, and we talk about them extensively throughout this book. A goal is something that we want to have or achieve that is concretely defined.

"I want to lose 20 pounds before my birthday next year." This is a concrete goal that has a well defined and understood objective and a desired time of completion. There's no discussion of whether I need to lose the weight, or whether or should, or why I want to achieve that milestone by this particular upcoming birthday.

Ambitions are similar to goals in that they describe something that we want to be or achieve but in an abstract manner. We are working with ambitions in the book as well, though you may not have made the connection yet, as I prefer to use the terms vision or purpose to describe the abstract targets that drive a team forward.

"I'm going to work to be in the best shape of my life." This is an excellent ambition because it is aspirational, abstract, but not too abstract such that it defies further definition. I can easily understand this ambition, and work to break it down further into concrete goals that will help me achieve it.

Values are the beliefs we hold that we consider unquestionable. They are the fundamental truths we hold to be self-evident. The reference to the United States Declaration of Independence is, of course, intentional.

Our personal values can often be hard to explain to others because, for each of us, they are usually not concepts that we naturally consider subject to logical or rational explanation. We believe our values, we believe *in* our values, and they are so ingrained in who we are that we consider them unquestionable tenants. They are so fundamental to who we are, we feel they should be evident to everyone.

Of course, not everyone has the same values. When our values clash individually, hopefully, we have a logical discussion where we may try to rationalize our value system to someone else, and we may end by saying, "We'll just have to agree to disagree." At the other end of the spectrum, we clash on a global scale. We see the outcomes of these every time we read or watch the world news.

When we are at our best, however, our values both define us and guide us to be who we believe we should be. We inherit some of these from our families, our social circles, our religious beliefs, and our societies. Others are entirely our own. The unique combination of values we adopt forms the core of our personality and who we become.

I include the description of goals and ambitions along with values here as I find it both interesting and useful to help us understand people, fictional or otherwise. If you have never worked through a value discovery exercise, you may find it difficult to approach at first, certainly more so if the facilitator begins by asking you, "What are your values?"

By understanding goals and ambitions, we can instead start by asking ourselves more straightforward questions, and then working deeper. Something like, "Tell me a goal you have right now, that you want to achieve relatively soon. Make it something concrete, and near term."

Any of us can generally supply something, even if we just fall back on our most recent New Year's resolutions.

Working backward from that goal, we can ask ourselves why we want to have that particular thing or reach that accomplishment.

Once we understand the abstract motivation that inspired us enough to set a goal — even if we didn't keep it — then we can continue the introspection, asking why again until we have eliminated all of the abstract, logically explainable reasons.

When we've done that when we can dig no deeper, and our response to repeated ask, "Why?" is simply "Because it's important to me."

Then we've reached our values.

At the end of this chapter, you'll find a value discovery exercise that walks you through this exercise. The concepts here are inspired by multiple resources for fiction writers. I've included links in the footnotes if it's something that intrigues you as much as it does me.[4]

Setting Your Goals

Now let's talk about goals.

I have found that when looking back on any 5-year plan, my progress is unrecognizable from where I started, or where I thought I would end up.

Often, the only constant in life is change.

But, I'm also a person that believes you need those goals, that driving purpose, regardless of the historical outcomes.

Whatever length of time works for you, whether it's a month, a quarter, a year, or a 5-year plan — I want you to set yourself goals that will encourage you to continue to improve and grow as a leader, and hopefully as a person.

What is measured will improve. Don't let your ability as a leader go unmeasured.

Keep your values in mind, and make a conscious effort to choose goals that are inherently more achievable because they are well aligned to your values.

Consider not only how you want to improve yourself, but how you can develop as a resource and mentor to your team, and the people around you that may not be on your team, but need your leadership or guidance just the same.

Set goals that require you to leverage your time more effectively, increase the value your leadership brings to your team, and that support your long term direction and aspiration for your career and your life.

Take Action

Goals without action are just dreams. A vision board without a plan to achieve it is just a pretty collage.

Execute. Move forward. Do something everyday that pushes you closer to achieving what you want.

I believe that you deserve to achieve the things that you want, if and when you want them strongly enough to take action.

So take action. You'll get some things right. Others you'll get wrong.

Yes, you will fail.

Learn from those failures. Push forward despite them, because you know that you only really fail when you quit.

Most importantly, be who you want to be. Be that person today, not tomorrow. And be honest with yourself about who that is, what your values are, and how the two align.

Without a plan to move forward, at best, you will stay right where you are. Leadership requires both intentional thoughts, and deliberate action; your professional development requires nothing less.

———

Leaders Take Action

I want you to inventory your current personal or professional development goals. Feel free to use a mix of both. Spend 10 minutes and write out either goals you have currently, or new goals you want to adopt. Remember: goals are concrete, measurable, and time-bound. You don't have to get this perfect, just push yourself to get it done. If you have extra time on the clock, challenge yourself to dig deeper and come up with a few more.

Example:

I want to lose 20 pounds by July 1st.

I want to build a collection of mechanical timepieces over the next 5 years.

I want to travel to a new country next year.

Now, take your goals list and start a new list. On this list, I want you to identify your ambitions, your vision, or purpose statements. These should be abstract, but clear in your mind. If you can visualize the destination or achievement and think, "I'll know it when I get there." — that's about right. Start by listing any that come to mind immediately. Now go back to your goal sheet, and for each goal, you listed, write the ambition or ambitions that are driving you to want to achieve that goal. It's okay to have more than one ambition per goal and also okay if you have more than one goal per ambition. Ask yourself why you want to reach that achievement or have that thing that the goal identifies. Why is it important to you? Why do you want it? Take another 10 minutes here.

Example:

As I get older, I want to achieve and maintain the best health and fitness of my life.

I want to see and experience as much of the world as possible.

For the next exercise, take 5 minutes and review your goals and ambitions. If you find any goals that you cannot relate back to your at least one ambition, question how committed you are to that goal. Should it be included? Do you really want it? Remove anything that doesn't make the cut.

Example:

Losing weight is related to my ambition to maintain excellent health and fitness as I get older.

My watch collection isn't related to any ambition I felt strongly about, so it doesn't make the list.

My plan to travel to a new country next year is related to my ambition to see and experience the world.

Okay, next, I want you to stack rank your ambitions, so they are ordered from the most important to the least important. You can do this easily by looking at the list and asking, "Which of these am I most excited about or want to achieve the most?" Move that item to the top of the list, and then repeat the question until the original list is empty and all items are ordered. Take 5 minutes to complete this. No need to overthink it.

Example:
　Maintain my health and fitness
　Travel the world

Finally, it's time to discover your values. Start from your ranked ambitions list. For each item on the list, you identified that ambition by asking yourself why it is important to you. Now I want you to ask why you value the achievement or thing you identified as abstractly important to you. If you are struggling with this, then complete the following sentence: I want to <ambition> because nothing is more important than <value>.

As you can see from the examples below, you don't have to follow this rigorously — it's merely a tool to direct your thoughts and find your values.

Example:
Health and Happiness
I want to maintain my health and fitness, because nothing is more important than living a happy life, and when my health is not taken care of, my happiness suffers.
Communication and Experiences
I want to travel the world because nothing is more important than experiencing and learning about other people and places, which helps us communicate and understand each other better.

19

INVESTING IN PROFESSIONAL DEVELOPMENT

"If you are not willing to learn, no one can help you. If you are determined to learn, no one can stop you." [1]

— ZIG ZIGLAR

Effective leadership requires a commitment to ongoing personal and professional development.

In the last chapter, we discussed your core values and the need to both establish goals and take action if you want to continue to grow as a leader. If you followed the framework we used to in the chapter on planning for success, your long term plan should be centered around a well-understood team purpose, that is then broken down into objectively measurable goals for near term planning and execution.

Often when we start thinking about the future we want to achieve, we tend to focus primarily on objective outcomes. What is the next promotion that we want? What new business objectives do we want to hit in the next year? What expectations do I need to meet?

Starting from those goals, it's not unreasonable to expect that we develop a plan that focuses on actionable steps that will take us from where we are to where we need to be.

While this is both a reasonable and commendable course of action, I'd like you to take a pause here and ensure that as you focus on realizing your goals, you don't lose sight of the need to invest in your professional development consistently over time.

To help you do that, we're going to expand your plan to ensure it includes consistent work on your professional development, which will, in turn, support and promote the successful achievement of your objective team goals.

As an individual contributor, your performance was likely measured by your output. Create more, process more, achieve more. As a leader, at a superficial level, at least, you will often be judged solely by the output of your team. You must find an effective way to affect that output.

While you can continue to set goals and rely on your grit, determination, and general scrappy-ness to keep meeting goals — there is a more straightforward path. And, it is a path that helps us avoid some management pitfalls, like falling back into a hands-on, do-it-yourself mode.

If you focus purely on demanding higher output from your team, and you add nothing else of value, I have bad news for you.

You are not leading, but managing.

In that scenario, you effectively assign the responsibility for improvement to the individual members of your team, where it rightly belongs. But, if you aren't doing anything material to guide and encourage the growth that you demand, you are failing in your role not just as the leader of your team but as a functional resource that plays a crucial role in supporting the team's success.

The practice you can adopt to avoid this is to commit the time necessary to invest in your own professional development and growth.

How does your development help your team?

As the team's leader, one of your principal responsibilities is personnel development. You need to encourage ongoing growth, help each person increase their value to the organization, and assist them in meeting their career goals.

Ironically, you can best achieve this by taking the time to continue to develop yourself.

The foundation of all leadership is not the work the team does, but the people. Improving your ability to relate to, communicate with, and inspire people will do more to affect your ability as a leader than any technical or domain knowledge you may possess.

Consider topics for improvement, such as:

- **Communication Skills:** Can you communicate effectively and efficiently, getting your thoughts, ideas, and expectations across to your team?
- **Conflict Resolution and Mediation:** How do you react to, evaluate, and resolve conflict on your team or between teams within your organization?
- **Creativity:** Can you improve your ability to produce or guide the team towards creative solutions to problems?
- **Mindfulness and Focus:** Are you often distracted or lacking focus?
- **Coaching and Mentoring:** Can you improve your ability to mentor your team's ongoing growth?

Anyone in business that aspires to gradually higher levels of authority would also benefit from at least a basic understanding of contract law. At some point, you may be required to read, understand, and potentially edit and execute a non-disclosure, non-compete, or other similar legal documents. Even if you only leverage it to understand employment agreements, either your own or those you issue to your team, your time investment will prove useful.

Spend time learning high level or abstract concepts related to the areas of expertise required by your team. I have not found a more effective means of establishing a bond and strong working relationship with a team as demonstrating and interest and level of capability with the work that consumes their day.

Does this mean you have to be able and willing to "get your hands dirty" or achieve a particular level of mastery? No, not necessarily. But, you do need to be able to demonstrate to your team that you have a real interest and respect for their work and areas of expertise. Your time investment in professional growth development can deliver this. The additional value you'll bring to team discussions, and collaborative work sessions also can't be overstated.

Practicing and encouraging an ongoing commitment to development positions you as a leader, both by setting a positive example, as well as providing yourself and your team directly with the skills and knowledge they need to effect meaningful improvement.

Inspiring growth and development in others, particularly in the people on your team, comes most naturally when leading by example.

"Do as I say, not as I do" is not a viable strategy for effective leadership, and I would argue that in the long term, it will fail you in a pure management role as well.

Make a point to explain the "why" or purpose behind your behaviors and choices related to professional development. This can be difficult if its a new concept for you in discussions with your team, but as you get more comfortable with incorporating these discussions into your regular interactions, you should find that it gets easier and feels more natural. Often a discussion about the purpose of the team, an objective goal, or a professional development milestone may provide that point of common understanding that helps people relate to their own experiences and behaviors.

Instructions or orders that are given without explanation or opportunity for discussion occasionally work with children and pets, but outside of that have more limited applicability, certainly so when considering how you interact with your team.

Your role as a leader will require you to learn and grow and encourage your team to do the same. Your value as a leader is directly correlated to your ability to continue guiding your organization to new heights of achievement, and this requires investment in personal and professional development.

This book is a start to change your mindset, change your habits, and set you on the path, but it is only *a start* — don't stop here.

Leaders Take Action

- *Brainstorm 5 areas of focus where you feel you'd most benefit from ongoing professional development.*

- *Stack rank the topics you've identified from the most impactful to the least impactful.*
- *Considering both your core values and your approach to time management, create a professional development plan for yourself that commits time every week to the development of the most impactful topic listed above. Time-box the activity to ensure it's focused, long enough to be effective, and short enough to avoid interruption or rescheduling.*
- *Review your development plan periodically, and evaluate whether your most impactful topic has shifted due to your efforts. Adjust your strategy accordingly.*
- *Brainstorm 5 ideas that you can implement to encourage your team to prioritize professional development. Bonus points if you can do so without assigning it as a quarterly, annual, or another formal goal.*

20

DEVELOP YOUR BOARD OF ADVISORS

"Leadership is the other side of the coin of loneliness, and he who is a leader must always act alone. And acting alone, accept everything alone."[1]

— FERDINAND MARCOS

L eadership is often described as a lonely endeavor, and we will usually be required to make decisions for which we alone will be held accountable. This absolute acceptance of responsibility is commendable. But, it can also lead us toward an unnecessary risk of failure if we take the concept of sole responsibility too far.

The error we often make is in failing to ask for help.

Not help from your team, though I would encourage you to seek their advice in their respective areas of expertise. Doing so communicates respect for that person's knowledge and experience. It's also a necessary tool for anyone that wishes to lead their team to higher-order achievements, those objective goals that can only be reached by the coordinated application of different expert skill sets toward solving a common problem.

No, in this case, what I'm referring to is the burden of leadership itself. Where can you turn when you need advice or guidance to assist you with navigating and understanding the unique challenges of leadership?

You need a **Board of Advisors**. A board of advisors, in this context, is a virtual peer group where you can seek (and give) advice that helps you solve distinct challenges or grow in particular problem areas as you advance as a leader.

Napoleon Hill, the late author most famous for his book **Think and Grow Rich**, published an earlier series of pamphlets entitled: **The Law of Success in Sixteen Lessons**. These pamphlets were initially released in 1925, and then later edited and rebound into a single printed volume in 1928.[2]

In his books, Hill introduces the concept of a "Master Mind" or "Master Mind Alliance" — what we now generally refer to as a mastermind group.

The idea is simple yet profoundly valuable. When two or more committed and intelligent individuals come together to exchange and explore ideas or thoughts — a meeting of the minds — they actually form a third virtual entity. A Master Mind.

Put another way, when we act alone, by definition, we lack perspective. As much as we may try to be unbiased in our thoughts and actions as leaders, when actively in complete solitude, we simply cannot replicate the valuable perspective we would receive from discussion with a peer.

I don't want to imply that the advice you receive is limited to perspective. Where your available peers operate in the same domain and can offer more prescriptive advice, of course, you should consider it. But, in any scenario, and regardless of business or market you are in, your peer board of advisors can always offer you perspective.

Perspective is powerful. Often we already possess the knowledge or experience we need to make a decision or solve a particular leadership challenge. We may not, however, realize that we have the solution to our current problem if we lack the perspective necessary to put the appropriate pieces together.

Our biases or other mental blocks prevent us from getting out of our own head and looking at the problem from a different angle.

And, sometimes, we just need someone that can tell us when we are being stubborn, unfair, or just plain stupid. Hearing this type of advice from someone you respect, in a time and place that leaves you free to make corrections is the much more natural, if often more humbling path.

Before we get into specific considerations while building your board of advisors, there's an important point you need to realize.

Just as you will find situations where you want to receive advice, so will other leaders in your inner circle need your help.

Yes, this road to leadership enlightenment is a two-way street. If you want to maintain the relationships you will call on to form your board of advisors over the long term, you must be prepared to offer advice, insight, and perspective to them as well.

Helping your peers in this way, even when they work in different areas, different markets, or completely different team and organizational structures is undoubtedly rewarding — who doesn't like the feeling they receive when they have genuinely helped someone else with a problem? But, the one thing that can be easy to overlook is that in helping your peers solve their leadership problems, it will force you to look harder at your own practices, and possibly improve yourself in the process.

Writing this book has been a similar experience for me. As I've worked on unpacking the things I've learned over the last few decades, I've had to shine a bright light on how I approach leadership from a practical perspective. But, I've also had to consider how I think about it and how I can better express those adopted principles to others.

Now that we're agreed on the equal exchange of value that will make your board of peer advisors viable for the long term, we need to determine how we fill those virtual seats.

Who do you choose to sit on your board of advisors?

Start with people from your network that you know, like, and trust. Diversity in areas of expertise and levels of relevant experience is also a valuable consideration, but keep this within an acceptable margin. Try to balance the relative areas of strengths or weaknesses across the small group of people you will gather. Keep the concept of the two-way street in front of your mind. Maintain the ability for the group to provide an even exchange of value between its members.

Next, think about accessibility. Do you have an existing relationship with the people you are considering that would support periodic discussions to exchange advice? If not, you'll either need to build those relationships or identify different people.

In terms of size, you'll find this varies based on your needs and personal preferences but recommend you start by identifying 3 to 5 people. I'm *a bit* of an introvert, so a smaller group really appeals to me. If you need or want a larger group of advisors, go for it. Just bear in mind that for each person that you want to have on your board so you can solicit their advice, you are also obligated to help them in return.

Now let's talk format. Again, this is something you can decide and adjust to best meet your needs. Exchanging contact details and agreeing to ad-hoc calls for advice is a viable, low impact way to start. You can arrange something as informal as an agreement to check-in individually or as a group in your chat application of choice. Or, you can establish a regular meeting cadence and a formal agenda — or anything in between.

As before, consider the group you are putting together and what will work best for everyone involved. You don't have to adopt the complete, formal mastermind structure, but I do recommend you incorporate some form of periodic group chat or meeting. Some topics — and some people — will work better in a one to one setting. But, the benefit of a group discussion is that everyone can both offer their perspective, as well as take away any relevant value to be applied to their own challenges.

Finally, as you think about how you will form your advisors and who you will ask to join, I want you to remember two things. This is not a competitive sport, and those virtual board seats are not granted for life.

Your goal in participating in the advisory group is not to determine who is a better leader, but to ensure the group is made better by the efforts of everyone in it.

At some point, you may find that one or more members of the group are not participating as expected or as much as they once were. Maybe one of those members is, in fact, you.

If you find someone struggling to have anything of value to offer to the members of the group, it may be time to cycle someone else from your network into that seat — or politely remove yourself if you are, in fact, the one who's growing more disconnected. Like anything else, this structure requires maintenance over time, and paying attention to that will ensure it remains valuable for everyone involved.

Being an effective leader is hard. People are both maddeningly complicated yet surprisingly simple, and will not fail to surprise you with their requests and needs. Often, what you will lack most in these situations is someone you can discuss your current challenge with, and solicit advice.

Develop your network of valuable relationships, both inside and outside your organization, and then formalize those relationships into a helpful, virtual mastermind group that offers something you can't buy anywhere else: perspective.

Leaders Take Action

- *Brainstorm 5 areas where you expect to need advice, that hour board of advisors will ideally provide.*
- *Brainstorm your initial list of people you want to consider for your board of peer advisors.*
- *Review the list you created. Is anyone too far above or below your experience level to effectively act as a peer? Remove them. Remember that effective peer relationships facilitate an equal exchange of value.*
- *Brainstorm 5 ways you will be able to help your advisors when they need you. Focus on your expertise*

or talents, particular in areas your proposed advisory group lacks.

- *Repeat the exercises above until you are confident that your list of advisors represents both a valuable resource for you, as well as a good mix of individuals that you can also advise.*

21

ENGAGE A MENTOR OR COACH

What do you do when you've built a peer group, a virtual board of advisors, but they cannot help with the challenges you face?

Having that board of advisors that you can consult regularly is exceptionally valuable, but it won't solve every problem.

While your peer group can provide critical input and perspective on specific challenges, it is a group of people founded on the principle of exchanging value. Remember that two-way street?

The group is also populated by people that are at least marginally within the same range of experience and level of professional development as you. Again, this enables that collaborative environment where the group can assist each other and ensure that everyone participating receives good value for their time spent.

As I am sure you are aware, each of these peers has demands on their time, just as you do. And, time is the one thing that always seems to be in short supply.

This creates a situation where those peers work well

when we need assistance or advice on specific problems. But, it doesn't work as well when we need help answering the broader questions that fall outside the scope of experience our peer group can offer. Put another way, your board of advisors should be well situated to advise what your next step toward solving a particular challenge should be. Still, they are unlikely to be able to help you determine the path you need to take to reach a goal that is 10 steps in the future.

Unless someone in your peer group is tackling the same or very similar challenges in their professional development, chances are good that you will need to look for another resource for assistance. Not just an additional person to assist, but another *type* of aid altogether.

You need someone that is a step or two ahead of you and by extension, a step or two ahead of your peers. Someone that has walked the path before you that can help you find your way.

The differences in the relationship you would typically establish with a coach or mentor are relevant as well. The coaching or mentoring relationship is quite different from the advisory relationship you will build and maintain with your peers in your virtual board. While a coach or mentor should be helping you to discover the answers you need, their approach to doing so will often be much more directive than the advice exchanged by your peers.

Where your peer advisors will offer suggestions, perspectives, and opinions whose purpose is to remove your biases and challenge your thinking, your coach or mentor will take more of a teaching role. They will instruct you directly in some cases, and guide you to the appropriate instruction in others.

If you enter into a mentoring relationship with one of the people in your circle of peer advisors, it could complicate the free flow of information and exchange of valuable advice between the two of you, and within the group as a whole.

The peer relationship is symbiotic, the coaching relationship is not. While it's certainly not impossible for the coach to learn from you in the process of coaching you — it's not the foundational purpose of the relationship. You expect to learn from the coach or mentor, there is no expectation that they must learn from you.

While this may be something you could possibly manage, I still wouldn't recommend finding your coach from within your virtual board of advisors. It comes back to the concept of perspective, coupled with experience. This is not a case where less is more. You want that new perspective and access to a wealth of additional knowledge that you don't currently possess.

Now that we've established that a professional coach or mentor will help you with the broader vision and focused planning, to ensure you are moving forward toward a clear destination, let's clear up any confusion between coaching and mentoring and determine which one you need.

What is the Difference Between a Coach or a Mentor?

The definition of the two can be unclear, depending on the source.

For our purposes here, we'll use mentoring to mean the formation of a professional relationship focused on overall development that is often either long term or entirely open-ended in scope.

Coaching, on the other hand, is generally more time-constrained and focused on specific results to be achieved within that defined time constraint.

Mentoring relationships are often established within the workplace, either with a manager or an assigned mentor — but this is not a hard rule. They can also be formed with an external mentor.

Coaching relationships are more often formed with an external person acting as the coach, usually in a paid capacity. Again, this is a generalization, as coaching will often be performed by a manager or a mentor, as coaching becomes the right tool to solve a given challenge.

Coaching is sometimes described as only focused on objective goals, whereas mentoring is solely focused on overall professional or personal development.

This is, in my opinion, something of a mischaracterization, as mentoring toward long term growth will often need to leverage a more coaching-oriented approach. Similarly, coaching someone to achieve a particular objective result will only be successful if the driving purpose behind the goal is well understood. This often requires the application of skills more closely associated with mentoring to establish.

So, Which One Do You Need?

If you need more general direction to establish your career progression objectives and identify your professional aspirations clearly, a mentor who can commit to developing a long term relationship with you as you evolve will be more beneficial.

If your goals or objectives are already well defined and you need help achieving those goals in a shorter period where the outcome will be objectively measurable, then you need a coach that can help you focus on achieving these goals.

In reality, you'll most likely need both at various times.

Ideally, you'll find someone that can act in both capacities. A hybrid that can shift smoothly between helping you identify your long term development direction and your short term, more tactical goals, and assist you in planning how you will accomplish them.

Beyond just asking for help when you need it, as a leader, you must have a long term plan that is built from a clear vision and founded on well-understood goals.

You need to align that plan to your personal and professional values. Your plan should help articulate how you will get to the future you envision for yourself, it shouldn't arbitrarily change the destination completely.

Forming that plan can be a daunting task, but with the right perspective and guidance to help you break down this seemingly complex problem into actionable steps, you'll get there.

The coaches and mentors you leverage along the way will see to it.

———

Leaders Take Action

- *Do you feel you need more assistance setting longer-term direction and goals, or shorter duration, highly focused work to achieve a particular result?*
- *Brainstorm and list 5 areas of focus, or specific results that a coach or mentor could help you achieve.*

22

PREPARE YOUR TEAM TO REPLACE YOU

"As we look ahead into the next century, leaders will be those who empower others."[1]

— BILL GATES

Developing a leadership style that focuses on developing your team to be successful is not a new concept, but it remains one that is not necessarily common.

What if I told you that your ultimate accomplishment as a leader is to create a team that no longer needs you? That can be a frightening prospect if you've never considered it before.

If you make yourself irrelevant, what does that mean for your future?

What's next for you if your current role no longer requires you to fill it?

You may have a career progression in mind that you are actively pursuing, or you may not. In either case, we don't often think about the void we will leave behind when we are ready to move on. We look forward to the future. Doing so allows us to plan that upward move on our own terms.

We can plan for it and take definitive action to give us the best chance of reaching it. Ultimately we have some control over the journey to our chosen destination. There are few certainties in life, but with a reasoned approach, we can put ourselves in the driver's seat.

When we turn that around and consider moving out of our role because we are no longer needed there, it just *feels* different. It feels like a loss of control, and in a way, it is.

In the first scenario, you focus on your own development and the feedback you receive that helps you understand your progress towards and readiness for a move up or out of your current role.

In the latter scenario, your level of control feels more tenuous. What if your team develops quicker than planned? What if they are ready to assume your responsibilities before you are prepared to move on? What if they are better than you?

Let it go.

Don't let your fear of the unknown, or your reaction to a perceived loss of control cause you to hold back in your efforts to develop your team.

Doing so is a disservice to you and to them.

Instead, shift your focus to one of developing your team without limitation, and recognize that your own development will not stop or slow in the least.

You see, as you focus on developing your team, you'll quickly realize that the things each person struggles with on their own path to improvement are different. Their challenges will not always be similar to your challenges. And, as a leader, you will have to dynamically figure out how to best coach them through those challenges. You will learn as you teach. And, your knowledge and expertise will expand in ways you may not have explored if not for the opportunity to assist with someone else's unique challenges.

You will have to set aside any fear of becoming irrelevant and adopt transparency and willingness to share the responsibilities that will provide an opportunity for your team first to understand and then start to assume parts of your role.

Yes, this means you need to focus on developing your team to be leaders themselves.

Does everyone want to lead? No. A typical response to this question is that not everyone *can* lead.

I disagree.

Tony Robbins said, "Change is never a matter of ability, it's always a matter of motivation."[2]

Not everyone has the innate ability that makes them a natural leader, but everyone does have the capability if they are motivated to do the work necessary.

Whether they choose to pursue that path will be a choice, each person has to make on their own. Will they commit to the changes and growth necessary to assume a leadership role?

"Change is inevitable, growth is optional."[3]

— JOHN C. MAXWELL

It is our job as leaders to identify those individuals on our team that have potential as future leaders. And, once we've found them support their development as leaders and individuals, without reservation.

You earned your leadership role by exemplary accomplishments as an individual contributor. You worked hard to excel in your role and in doing so, achieved a position of accountability, responsibility, and authority. You either chose a leadership role, or it chose you — either way, you committed to becoming the leader the position requires.

Doing so likely required you to reshape your priorities, re-evaluate your skills, and plot a path to be successful in a new environment.

You may not have a vision for what comes next, and not knowing what lies in store for you may make you hesitant to grow your team to the point you become irrelevant.

There was likely a point in time in your role as an individual contributor where you also couldn't see a clear path into management. You may not have had an interest in moving into management at all. What changed your mind, or allowed you to start seeing the possibility of an eventual move to management?

Did the shift occur as you started establishing yourself more as a peer leader? Or, was it something you realized as your career progressed?

Recognize that as you develop yourself as a leader to support and grow your team, you will also develop new and expanded skills that open opportunities that require those additional skills.

A common adage says, "when the student is ready, the teacher appears." Similarly, when you are ready, new opportunities will appear.

Have you ever had a thought or idea that you dismissed almost immediately as lacking in some way? Maybe it is a creative undertaking, a new project, or a hobby you'd like to take up. Your logical mind and creative mind can't agree on the specifics, and you quickly set it aside.

We all do this. It's how we attempt to focus as we are

surrounded by a world of distractions. We are subconsciously trying to identify and focus on the things that matter most at any given time.

This same subconscious filter can work against us by blinding us to opportunities that are not clearly aligned with our own self-identified plans. We inadvertently develop tunnel vision, as we hyper-focus on our well-understood goals.

This is not, in and of itself, a bad thing — but as we assume responsibility for the success and growth of a team of people, don't let this behavior prevent you from being successful in that role as a coach, mentor, and leader simply because you can't see your next opportunity.

You can't see the forest for the trees.

Fear of the unknown is natural, but as leaders, we must have the courage to choose our actions despite our concerns, not because of them.

You can start by sharing progressively more of the responsibilities of leadership in a controlled manner with the people on your team. Identify those individuals that show interest or excel in critical areas and start to develop them to assume an appropriate subset of your responsibilities.

Do this gradually, and in a way that evaluates and respects their growing skills. Continue to make sensible and reasoned decisions, while assessing your own motivations for those decisions to ensure you are not acting defensively out of fear.

Finding a way to abstract yourself out of the team is the ultimate example of transformative leadership. When you successfully achieve it, you will have proven an ability to evolve the team enough to replicate and replace the value you bring.

In the process, you will grow your own value and open yourself to opportunities that were once unimaginable.

———

Leaders Take Action

- *Consider your current team, and the gaps in experience or skills they have that would prevent them from replacing you.*
- *Could you fulfill your role if two or more people on the team shared your responsibilities?*
- *Brainstorm 5 ways you could start to close some of the skills gaps that are preventing the people on your team from moving into your role.*
- *Consider the different strengths and weaknesses of everyone on your team. How can you leverage the team's strengths such that they help each other improve?*
- *Delegate your responsibilities to your team on a limited basis, such as when you go on vacation. Use these occurrences to evaluate their progress, and help them more comfortable with your job. Plus, you get to go on vacation.*
- *If you know what your next desired career move is, document it. If you don't brainstorm some ideas about what it could be.*
- *Are you ready to move into that position today? If someone on your team excelled enough to take over your job, what would your gaps be before you were prepared to assume one of your dream roles?*
- *Brainstorm 5 things you can add to your professional*

development plan that will close the gaps that prevent you from assuming your next desired role or position.

23

DEVELOP A CULTURE OF CONTINUOUS IMPROVEMENT

I want you to build an unstoppable, fantastic team. The surprising truth is we never really arrive at some point and say, "We've made it!"

The more you and your team successfully achieve, the more will be expected of you. Of course, the rewards and satisfaction from a job well done, from accomplishments reached, continues to grow as well.

Leadership is a journey that requires ongoing investment and maintenance.

As leaders, we forge a path for our teams and the people around us. By walking a few steps ahead, we can show the way forward, and inspire those around us to reach higher. We chart a path for others to follow in our footsteps, and eventually, they surpass us as they lead the way forward for others.

What happens if we stop?

I don't mean what happens when you retire, or just decide you don't like your job, so you aren't going to go anymore, like Peter in Office Space.[1]

What happens if we stop improving?

If we stop improving, or we stop learning, we lose our ability to lead.

Ironically, in a way only Mike Judge could pull off, Peter managed to stop working, and continue to lead — though probably not in a direction we want to emulate. As funny as I find it, I can't in good conscience suggest that you lead your team into a life of crime.

Self Improvement

You have a responsibility as a leader to demonstrate a commitment to continuous improvement that challenges you to grow and improve over time. In doing so, you will both set an example, and hopefully, directly challenge your team to improve, to learn from mistakes, and perform at a higher level as they gain experience in their roles and as a unit.

The example you set, when consistently reinforced by mentoring and support, will do more to inspire decisive action from your team than any directive guidance alone.

We've already discussed the need for professional development: the continuing investment in expanding the knowledge and skills you bring to the team, both in your role as a leader, and to support the various individual areas of expertise needed by your team. What we will focus on here is expanding that development plan in a few additional key areas that should directly enable you to improve team processes and output.

The specific improvements you pursue, of course, will differ based on your situation, your business, market, and job function. Still, these suggested areas of focus will help you expand your professional development plan. Adding targeted skills for improvement that demonstrate to your team that you not only invest in your professional development but in growing your ability to lead your team to success more effectively.

You will never regret, nor should you ever neglect, ongoing investment in developing your soft-skills. As we have covered those in our previous chapter on professional development, we won't repeat them here. As you expand your development plan, however, make sure you don't let your attention to soft skills slip.

I offer the suggestions below in no particular order, draw from each as you see fit, or where you feel you have the most pressing need.

Domain Skills

The first area where you can easily add value as a leader is to expand your knowledge of the skills and areas of expertise required by your team.

In particular, you should focus on establishing a base knowledge in those areas where you are not already an expert. The benefit is you improve your conversations with your team beyond the topics of accountability and management of work. Your knowledge, experience, and expertise in your own areas of specialty will often lend itself to the generation of new ideas, or varying perspectives that help the team solve problems.

Parallels between different skills, areas of study, or even solutions to problems that seem unrelated, can often produce unconventional or unexpected positive results. A differing perspective, coupled with the basic knowledge necessary to add value to the conversation, can be the difference between finding a successful solution, or not.

You may not gain enough knowledge to participate in

problem-solving activities with your team materially. In some fields, it is just unreasonable to expect this. Still, your investment in time and energy to learn more about the team's area of expertise will demonstrate the respect you have for what they do, and further reinforce the positive relationships you want to build with each person.

Industry or Market Knowledge and Processes

It can be surprising to learn that industry or market knowledge is not always a universal requirement of every role on a team.

Let me give you a concrete example from my own experience. I lead a team of Product Managers responsible for delivering a successful cloud-based Software-as-a-Service (SaaS) product for the healthcare market.

None of my team, including me, has any background in healthcare beyond being a consumer.

We can solve problems for the market by focusing on using our skills as product managers to understand the problem and define the solution in the context of a healthcare market without necessarily needing to have a deep understanding of the healthcare aspects of the problem.

This works because problems solved by software tend to be similar across industries — and I expect this is not a phenomenon limited to software.

That being said, you will always benefit by taking a more active approach to learning about the industry or market where your team operates.

Am I going to return to school and become a doctor? No, and I'm not suggesting you should either — unless that's something you want to do. But, expanding my knowledge of the healthcare processes and domain language that will be directly relevant in much of the work my team and I do will continue to deliver benefits.

Team Improvement

As critically important as it is, self-improvement is only the first step. You have a responsibility as a leader to establish a culture of continuous improvement that challenges and encourages those around you to continue to grow and improve over time.

Complex goals or projects can be daunting. If we set goals that are too far from our current capabilities or reality, they can feel unattainable. This includes when we challenge our team to expand their skills and abilities.

We need to both remember and help our team understand that complicated things are really just a mass of smaller problems that have gotten tangled up together. Often we fail to recognize the small problems altogether. We can't see the more minor issues because they are disguised as a massive, tangled mess.

Help your team see this by setting realistic goals that are both valuable and attainable with committed, potentially hard work — but work that is achievable and within reach. Untangle something small and solve it first.

Game designers have a concept that is often described as hard fun. It is the idea that the enjoyment a player receives from the game is often directly correlated to the work they put into a particular achievement. If we receive something desirable or valuable, but we did little to attain it, we don't appreciate it. When we have to exert more effort, challenge ourselves to push beyond what is comfortable, and then achieve something, that achievement holds more meaning for us.

The challenge and effort involved actually impact the scope and scale of the reward. Keep this in mind as you challenge the team to improve. You want to strike a balance that gives meaning to the achievements they will reach, without setting the bar so high that the goals seem unobtainable.

A straightforward approach to doing so comes from James Altucher. We introduced this concept earlier in the book, but it bears repeating here.

James suggests that we simply try to improve 1% every day. Ask your team to develop some essential skill, process, or outcome by 1% day over day and compounded over time, the results will be monumental. Of course, defining what 1% means is up to you, and highly dependent on what exactly you are trying to improve. The key here is that your team doesn't need to try to boil the ocean. Solve something small today. Repeat that effort tomorrow, and the next day.[2]

Help your team think about how to break significant problems down into manageable tasks and then evaluate and prioritize those tasks effectively so they can focus on improving in the areas that will have the most impact.

As you focus on promoting improvement across the team, remember that you have two complementary approaches you can leverage: working with the team as a group and working with the individuals one on one. Don't limit your discussion of improvement too often to one approach or the other. Strike a balance between individual coaching and group discussion and activities.

The benefit of one on one coaching is that you allow each individual to speak freely and discuss their potential weaknesses or areas where they need assistance, including those that they may not be comfortable sharing with the larger group.

Group improvement, on the other hand, offers the benefit that it promotes accountability as the team is aware of each other's improvement efforts and can then act together to support and encourage one another.

As you work to develop your team's culture of improvement, ensure that you anchor the overall effort to your team's mission and the purpose or vision of the organization. Without meaningful inspiration, we lose motivation, and then we lose engagement. This is what solidifies the team culture. Bringing the team together to improve both individually and as a unit, to focus on shared responsibility.

Finally, you mustn't position yourself as the sole person who leads all growth and development on the team. Encourage the team to support and encourage that development in a peer to peer fashion. Not only will this promote growth in additional areas as each person champions those things that most interest or excite them, but it also ensures that growth can continue and even accelerate without your constant attention.

Organizational Improvement

We've now come full circle. In Part 1, we established a common understanding of culture and discussed how culture is an organic entity that is continuously changing.

As you develop your team culture, it will affect the culture of your organization. The reach and scale of that effect will depend on the organization, but some impact is all but inevitable.

Knowing the impact your team culture will have on the organizational culture, you have a responsibility as a leader to drive the business closer to achieving its goals, realizing its mission and exemplifying its core values.

Leadership starts with self-leadership. You must look after your own continued development. Leadership will allow you to shape and guide your team, and you must look after your team's continued growth. And leadership does not stop at the boundaries of your team. You also need to play a role in driving a culture of improvement within your organization.

This may sound like a lot to ask, especially if you are new to management and just getting comfortable with thinking of yourself as a leader.

In his book **The Goal**, Eliyahu Goldratt introduces the Theory of Constraints.[3]

The book is a great "business novel" that explores productivity and throughput using a fictional story to present a series of key management concepts. Core among them is that the achievement of goals is typically limited by a finite number of constraints.

Identifying and removing those constraints is your path to success.

We discussed the need to guide your team to unravel their personal and group improvement challenges into small solvable tasks. This is nothing more than identifying the constraints that are limiting their growth.

This understanding of constraints does not just apply to your team internally but to the organization as a whole. Consider your team as an organism within the business. Your team has dependencies on other groups with their own missions, all aligned to the organizational objectives.

Within those relationships lie new constraints that can hinder or facilitate the successful achievement and growth of your team, and of the organization.

A chain is only as strong as its weakest link.

As a leader, you need to help identify where problems in

your organization may work against you as you improve your team. This will require you to develop into an omnidirectional manager. You may have heard of the concept of managing up, where you take an active approach to driving results not just with your own team, but with your manager and senior leadership. I suggest you expand that even further. I want you to manage up, down, and sideways. Don't neglect the need to lead your own peers, other managers within the organization, when the opportunity presents itself.

The challenge you need to be prepared for is the limitations transformational change of your team may experience if the organizational state is ignored. Don't let your team perform all the hard work necessary to achieve something amazing and have it fall apart because the pace of change has separated them from the rest of the organization. This can happen when we overlook the dependency relationships between our team and others within the organization or the organization itself.

The organization needs to move together. Different teams may do so at a different pace. Still, as long as those teams are inter-dependent on each other, we need to pay attention to any distance this creates between them, or the ability for those teams to work together effectively may break down.

Often, we can achieve this by taking the practices we've developed to improve our team and expand it out to the broader organization. Simply put, leadership by example, shouldn't stop at the boundaries of your team.

Find ways to demonstrate how and why your team is improving to the rest of the organization, and make it clear that you are open to discussing how your team has solved various challenges.

Obviously, this won't be specific to work being done, as more often than not, other groups are working on entirely different objectives that require different skill sets. Instead, share developments in management techniques you've learned or created and applied to your team. Share process improvements your team develops, where they may apply to another group. Share approaches to one on one management, and enhancements to soft skills that you discover with other managers who seem to be struggling with a similar problem.

Seek out the leaders of other teams in your organization and learn from them. As you seek their advice, they, in turn, will usually be more receptive to receiving input from you.

Just as your team cannot be successful by relying on the efforts of one or a small subset of individuals within the group, your organization is unlikely to be successful based on the efforts of one team alone.

Developing a culture of continuous improvement, where we embrace growth and necessary change will support your team, and your organization in any mission they choose to pursue. As we promote and work towards a state where the pursuit of excellence is the norm, we create an environment where we hold each other accountable for achieving it.

Leadership is a journey of growth for individuals, teams, and organizations that will take us anywhere we want to go, and open opportunities we may have never expected.

As we reach the end of this book, I hope I have helped you find your path and inspired you in some small way for the journey ahead.

———

Leaders Take Action

- *Brainstorm 5 key activities or areas that your team could improve on that would have a measurable impact.*
- *Review the ideas you produced. Can they be broken down to something smaller, or more achievable? Repeat this process until the improvements can't be any simpler, or breaking them down further would remove any positive impact.*
- *Repeat this process with your team, guiding them, and sharing your ideas from above as necessary. Start implementing the items the team collectively feels are most valuable today.*
- *Brainstorm 5 ways you can start sharing and showing developments on your team with the rest of the organization.*

AUTHOR'S NOTES

NOVEMBER 15, 2019

I've always been an avid reader. When I was a kid and did something that got me in trouble, the one thing my parents would never take away was access to books. I could always read as much as I wanted.

I read a lot as a kid. Not because I was particularly bad! I just loved to read, and I still do to this day.

I've always had this somewhat odd compulsion to write. Not because I feel driven to create something, but because I've received so much the written word. At some point, I just started feeling like I should give something back.

So here you have it, my first attempt at giving back.

I decided on a topic and outlined this book in early 2019. As is typical for me, I then got distracted by a number of other things — all related to the book — that kept me away from the actual writing.

My outline at the time was solid. I was really feeling confident in what I had put together. My goal was to have the book written and published by the end of 2019.

As the year moved on, and realized that goal wasn't

going to hold if I didn't sit down and put hands to keyboard. Who knew that books didn't write themselves?

There are so many people selling the message that you can dictate a book in a weekend and then transcribe it and edit it. Publish your book by next week! That was never a consideration for me. The things I wanted to share with you were too important when I learned them, and too important for you.

I did, however, think that I knew my content so well, and had such a strong outline that I would be able to write *my* book pretty quickly.

At the end of the process, I did write the book reasonably quickly, but all things are relative. It wasn't as fast as I thought I could complete it.

Who knew, writing is *hard*.

I'm paraphrasing here, and the source of the quote is debated anyway, so I'll stick with attributing it to Hemingway.

Writing is easy, just sit at the desk and bleed.

There's something to that, something you can't understand until you've sat down and tried to turn a vision in your mind into something tangible in the world.

It turns out it's not easy to put ourselves on the page. But, that's exactly what we want, what we need to do, if we are to create the thing we set out to create.

I hope you enjoyed the book. As hard as it was to write, I enjoyed the process and I'll be writing more.

Maybe, I'll see you for the next book as well?

BEST,
   Matt

ACKNOWLEDGMENTS

This book would not have been possible without the ongoing support of many people.

My wife, Miranda, for her continual willingness to read my writing and give feedback, and to push me to get out of my own head and recognize the value of my own work.

My family; while they don't always understand what I'm doing on the computer all the time, they have always believed I would be successful, whatever the endeavor.

My colleagues past and present, that were willing to pick up the phone and talk to me about leadership and organizational culture. You've helped me as much as I hope I have helped you.

Special thanks in particular to Allwyn Das, Chris Geier and Damian Tamayo, who were all instrumental in helping me refine my thoughts and talk through ideas for this book.

The wonderful people I've had the honor of working with over the years. You can't lead unless someone is willing to trust you to set their path, and the teams I've worked with over the years have placed that trust in me. If they had not, this book, this philosophy if you will, would not exist.

I've always been an avid reader, and eventually decided I'd like to add writer and author to my personal bio. Like so many others, the time between making the decision to write, and actually putting hands to keyboard was long.

Life sometimes gets in the way.

When I decided I was ready to take this writing thing seriously, and the time was now, the mentor that I needed appeared.

Honoree Corder has been a coach, mentor and friend over the past year as I planned, structured and wrote this book. Without her continual support and encouragement, not only would this book not be finished, I may not have discovered how much I enjoy writing.

If you are a professional that feels like they have a book in their future, I can't recommend a better guide to the process than Honoree. You can find her at: https://honoreecorder.com.

Thank you all.

NEED HELP?

Knowing where to start or what step to take next can be really difficult.

If you've finished the book and come away feeling energized and excited about where you can take your team, but you just aren't sure where to start — I can help.

If you are ready to drive transformational change in your team or your organization, I'd love to have you on my mailing list for intentional leaders.

You can join my list to connect directly with me. You'll also get a free gift!

https://go.leadwith.vision/reader-offer

SPECIAL REQUEST

Thank you so much for spending your valuable time reading my book. I hope you loved it, and I genuinely appreciate you.

Can I ask a favor? Will you take a few minutes to leave an honest review on Amazon?.

Reviews like yours help authors like me reach our audience — we can't do it without you!

The link below will take you directly to the book page, where you can leave your review — thank you!

https://go.leadwith.vision/spts-amazon-book

ABOUT THE AUTHOR

Matthew Overlund writes non-fiction and coaches professional development for new (or not so new) managers at Leadership & Vision, where he helps amazing people realize a higher potential as they evolve from getting things done to making things happen.

When he's not writing, coaching, or generally masquerading as a code jockey, solutions architect, or product manager, Matt occasionally writes, thinks, reads, or talks about writing fiction — where understanding the characters on the page help him understand the characters in the world.

NOTES

1. Who are you?

1. https://www.nightingale.com/articles/the-strangest-secret/
2. https://en.wikipedia.org/wiki/Michael_Scott_(The_Office)#Personality_and_management_style
3. https://en.wikipedia.org/wiki/Bill_Lumbergh

2. What's the problem?

1. The concept was introduced by Joseph M. Jurand and based on the work of Italian Economist Vilfredo Pareto.
2. https://americanexpress.com/en-us/business/trends-and-insights/articles/applying-the-8020-rule-to-your-employees-1
3. https://www.azquotes.com/quote/875419

4. Leadership vs. Management

1. https://en.wikiquote.org/wiki/Grace_Hopper
2. https://hbr.org/2017/06/how-managers-drive-results-and-employee-engagement-at-the-same-time

5. Organizational Culture

1. https://www.hbo.com/silicon-valley
2. https://medium.com/s/the-big-disruption/the-big-disruption-36fbed0268cf

6. Leaders value focus

1. https://www.sciencemag.org/news/2010/04/multitasking-splits-brain
2. https://www.nirandfar.com/hooked/
3. https://www.psychologytoday.com/us/blog/brain-wise/201209/the-true-cost-multi-tasking

4. https://www.franklincovey.com/the-7-habits/habit-3.html

7. Leaders manage communication

1. https://fremont.edu/top-10-tips-for-effective-workplace-communication/
2. https://www.thebalancecareers.com/communication-skills-list-2063779
3. Jung, C. G., and Godwyn Baynes, H. (1921). Psychologische Typen. Zurich: Rascher.

8. Leaders take control of their time

1. https://www.google.com/calendar
2. https://english.oxforddictionaries.com/opportunity%20cost%5D

9. Leaders build influence

1. https://books.google.com/books?id=3_40fK8PW6QC&printsec=frontcover#PPT7,M1
2. http://english.oxforddictionaries.com/influence
3. [http://english.oxforddictionaries.com/influence]

10. Leaders create systems

1. Max-Planck-Gesellschaft. "Decision-making May Be Surprisingly Unconscious Activity." ScienceDaily. www.sciencedaily.com/releases/2008/04/080414145705.htm (accessed October 13, 2019)
2. Pareto, Vilfredo; Page, Alfred N. (1971), Translation of Manuale di Economia Politica ("Manual of political economy"), A.M. Kelley, ISBN 978-0-678-00881-2

11. Leaders own failure and share success

1. Scott, Ridley, and Callie Khouri. 1991. Thelma and Louise. United States: MGM-Pathe Communications Co.

12. Understanding motivation

1. https://quora.com

13. Plan for Success

1. https://en.wikipedia.org/wiki/SMART_criteria

14. Fail Forward

1. https://en.wikiquote.org/wiki/Mike*Tyson*
2. https://www.sun-sentinel.com/sports/fl-xpm-2012-11-09-sfl-mike-tyson-explains-one-of-his-most-famous-quotes-20121109-story.html
3. https://www.quora.com/How-can-I-compete-with-people-who-are-better-than-I-am-in-every-way/answer/James-Altucher?awc=15748_1571492992_05c9dbef5c547d398087fe7761f2996c&uiv=6&txtv=8&source=awin&medium=ad&campaign=uad_mkt_en_acq_us_awin&set=awin&pub_id=78888

18. Determine your path

1. https://www.forbes.com/sites/kevinkruse/2012/10/16/quotes-on-leadership/#54b32ccd2feb
2. https://www.goodreads.com/quotes/1339572-when-the-student-is-ready-the-teacher-will-appear-when
3. http://mentalfloss.com/article/500800/most-famous-anti-drug-ad-turns-30-any-questions
4. https://www.amazon.com/Creating-Character-Arcs-Masterful-Development-ebook/dp/B01M6VC68U

19. Investing in Professional Development

1. https://www.goodreads.com/quotes/1254382-if-you-are-not-willing-to-learn-no-one-can

20. Develop Your Board of Advisors

1. https://www.brainyquote.com/quotes/ferdinand_marcos_182463
2. https://archive.org/details/Law_Of_Success_in_16_Lessons

22. Prepare Your Team to Replace You

1. https://www.forbes.com/sites/kevinkruse/2012/10/16/quotes-on-leadership/#54b32ccd2feb
2. https://www.facebook.com/TonyRobbins/posts/change-is-never-a-matter-of-ability-its-always-a-matter-of-motivation-upwdallas/10152791131579060/
3. https://www.goodreads.com/quotes/81497-change-is-inevitable-growth-is-optional

23. Develop a Culture of Continuous Improvement

1. 1999, https://www.imdb.com/title/tt0151804/
2. https://www.quora.com/How-can-I-compete-with-people-who-are-better-than-I-am-in-every-way/answer/James-Altucher?awc=15748_1571492992_05c9dbef5c547d398087fe7761f2996c&uiv=6&txtv=8&source=awin&medium=ad&campaign=uad_mkt_en_acq_us_awin&set=awin&pub_id=78888
3. https://en.wikipedia.org/wiki/The_Goal_(novel)

Made in the USA
Columbia, SC
11 March 2020